On the

Inspirational stories of social entrepreneurs
transforming Africa

Thanks for your support!

ON
THE
UP

Nikki & Rob

Nikki & Rob Wilson

Published by Wripped
Oxford, United Kingdom

Published by Wripped Ltd
59 Aldrich Road,
Oxford OX2 7SU
www.wripped.org
2 4 6 8 10 9 7 5 3 1

Credits: *Gua, © Emmanuel Jal, Gatwitch Records*

ISBN: 978-0-9572027-0-2

Printed and bound in the UK by the MPG Books Group, Bodmin and
King's Lynn
Typeset by Ken Vail Graphic Design, Cambridge
Cover design by Pookage Hayes
Edited by Kathryn Eyers and James Maroney

Wripped are committed to a sustainable future. The book in your
hands is made from paper certified by the Forest Stewardship
Council.

Wripped is a company limited by guarantee in England and Wales,
company number 7945438.

On the Up supported by:

Wripped Publications

The book you are reading is the first publication by Wripped, a new social enterprise. Wripped passionately believes that access to a good quality education is the fundamental right of every person on this planet. Education, above all else, has the power to overcome poverty, empower and inspire citizens, drive growth and reduce illness and disease. Yet despite huge advances in enrolment in education across the developing world, educational resource provision has not kept pace. The lack of good quality, low cost resources still presents a significant financial barrier to many children attaining the best education. Wripped believes that the wealth of knowledge available in the 21st Century should be shared and available to all.

In the coming months and years, Wripped will aim to publish a range of titles aimed at addressing this need, as well as others. Like the entrepreneurs in this book, when we see a need, we will do all we can to address it. Focusing on the social value good publishing can have in a range of areas, we will aim to show the same inspiration and innovation, dogged determination and, hopefully, humour that the entrepreneurs in On the Up show throughout this book. We hope you will keep an eye on us, buy our books, or even become part of our network.

Wripped has been established by James Maroney and Rob Wilson. James is an educational publisher who has lived and worked in East Africa and published across the Middle East, East Africa and the Horn. Rob is a founding director of READ International, NoPC and On the Up.

Wripped: **www.wripped.org**

Dedicated to all aspiring changemakers

Contents

Conclusion

References

Foreword

In 2010, Rob and Nikki Wilson applied for a joint Fellowship to The Winston Churchill Memorial Trust. It was immediately clear on meeting these two exceptional young people that they had not only already achieved highly but would continue to do so. Their passion to mobilise other young people to initiate social change shone through. We were in no doubt that we should award a Churchill Fellowship to them both.

It is fitting that the Churchill Trust supported Rob and Nikki's journey through Africa. My great grandfather, Sir Winston Churchill, saw military service in Sudan and covered the Boer War as a correspondent, where he was captured and then escaped 300 miles across Boer territory. He would have wholeheartedly approved not only of Rob and Nikki's journey but also of the purpose behind it, being a keen social reformer himself.

Like the Wilsons he felt his time overseas benefitted him hugely, and it was in this spirit that, on his death, the Memorial Trust was established, with his prior approval, so that British citizens could learn and grow from such experiences and use them for the improvement of the country as a whole. Since its launch in 1965 the Winston Churchill Memorial Trust has enabled over 4500 Fellows to travel the world in this way, returning to make significant and beneficial changes in their own communities and beyond.

At the heart of Rob and Nikki's journey from Cape Town to Cairo was a quest to find people working to improve the lives of others in innovative and inspiring ways. As you read about the people they met and whose stories they tell, I challenge you not only to be inspired by the people and projects in Africa but also by the Wilsons themselves. The Churchill Trust is delighted to be able to claim them as Churchill Fellows and we look forward to following them over the coming years as their journey continues.

Randolph Churchill

March 2012

Winston Churchill Memorial Trust: **www.wcmt.org.uk**

Acknowledgements

First and foremost we of course want to thank all of the social entrepreneurs who kindly gave up so much of their precious time to share their stories with us for this book: Charles Maisel, Shona McDonald, Trevor Field, Betty Makoni, Marianne Knuth, Simon and Jane Berry, Peter Sinkamba, Bart Weetjens, Rakesh Rajani, Mary Kayitesi Blewitt, Alexander McLean, Laren Poole, David Kuria, Nick Moon, Erik Hersman, Emmanuel Jal, Raghda El Ebrashi, and Sherif el Ghamrawy. You answered all of our questions with honesty and welcomed us into your worlds.

We also want to thank and mention the handful of incredible social entrepreneurs we met but just didn't have space to feature: Tim Conibear in South Africa, founder of Isiqalo Foundation (www.isiqalo. org); Katherine van Wyk in South Africa, founder of The African Pulse (www.theafricanpulse.net); Paul Joynson-Hicks in Tanzania, founder of Wonder Welders, Dar es Salaam Goat Races, and Molly's Network (www.wonderwelders.org, www.goatraces.com, www.mollysnetwork. org); and Andy and Susie Hart in Tanzania, founders of Neema Crafts (www.neemacrafts.com). You can read their stories in full on our website (www.ontheup.org.uk). We strongly urge you to take a look.

Our thanks also go to Brian Dugdill for introducing us to the East Africa Dairy Development (EADD) project and to William Matovu for driving us miles across Uganda so that we could gain an insight into what this fascinating dairy co-operative initiative is achieving. The EADD project was a great example of how large international aid organisations can come together with major funding to transform farming at a grass roots level.

Thank you to The Winston Churchill Memorial Trust (WCMT) for your financial sponsorship, without which there is no way we could have afforded to take such a once in a lifetime journey. We particularly want to thank Winston Churchill's great grandson Randolph for writing our foreword, the Trust Secretary Julia Weston, and the Director General Jamie Balfour. We hope we can continue to contribute to the Fellowships Programme and support others seeking funding from WCMT.

Thank you also to the Vodafone Foundation for providing us with free internet access across Africa and for your sponsorship of our book launch. Again we particularly want to thank a select few: Lord Michael

Hastings, a Vodafone Foundation Trustee who has been a great support to Rob over the past few years and Andrew Dunnett the Director of the Vodafone Foundation.

Everyone we met on our journey showed us their hospitality but some went to extra special lengths to feed us, house us, and perhaps best of all, give us pretty much the only hot showers we had in months. Thank you to Jenny Ievins, Tony and Marketa Brennan, the whole Joynson-Hicks clan (Paul, Cat, Emma, Tommy and Sammy), Paul and Marianne Knuth, and to Sherif el Ghamrawy who hosted us in his beautiful eco-resort in Egypt just before our first wedding anniversary.

A small group of trusted friends, family members and colleagues spent their time during the Christmas and New Year break of 2011/12 reading our entire manuscript, providing feedback and most crucially lending us their kind words of encouragement. We owe a debt of thanks to Bethan Jones, Catriona Maclay, Mark Cheng and Jane Berry. We also want to show our massive appreciation for those who helped with the wider project: Julia King for your design skills and wonderful project logo, Tim De La Salle for working on our website, Kathryn Eyers for volunteering her editing skills, Sam Vail for the design and layout work, and to Pookage Hayes for the cover design and a very special thanks to James Maroney, co-founder of our publisher Wripped, for pulling it all together and making this book a reality.

Lastly, a personal thank you to our family who helped with some of the more practical challenges which come with taking an extended career break overseas. To Rob's mum Margaret for storing all of our belongings in her beautiful cottage in Kent and for acting as our UK Secretary. And also to Rob's dad Richard for housing us both on our return whilst we looked for our next jobs. Richard – we know we stayed for far too long but that's your fault for making us feel so comfortable in your lovely home.

Meet the Authors

Before you get stuck into our stories, we want to share a bit about ourselves and some of the influences which led us to dream up this journey.

Rob and Nikki at the start of their journey in front of Table Mountain, Cape Town

About Rob (by Rob)

Before I went to university I thought charity work was all a bit geeky. I got behind the easy stuff, like knocking on doors to raise money, but when it came to my gap year I couldn't comprehend why people would waste their time on volunteering projects. And so I spent six months doing the standard thing – drinking my way around the world and having an awesome time.

At university I had a great mix of mates and for once they weren't all lads. When Rachel, still a close friend today, convinced me to go with her to a meeting about a new charity book project I agreed to go for one reason only – 'Fit Nikki' from M block was going too! Aside from hopelessly trying to flirt, the meeting was actually not bad. And when they mentioned that volunteers could spend a summer in Tanzania, well then I got excited.

Immediately this whole idea of going to Africa sparked a plan. My best mate Tom and I decided we would drive from the UK to Tanzania in a Land Rover, fill it with condoms and get sponsorship from Durex. Africa needs condoms, right? Bless our hearts... how ignorant we were. Thankfully our plans faded but the dream of going on a big adventure to Africa did not.

Meanwhile, Nikki and I had started going out so keeping up appearances was essential. But by then, Tanzania Book Project (TBP) as it was called, was starting to get under my skin. I bought into the simple premise that UK schools have loads of books, Tanzanian schools have very few. Even better, Tanzania's education system is based on ours so our books are genuinely relevant and useful to young people there. So, why not recycle books no longer needed by UK schools?

Loving the new role of 'man with a van' we drove to dozens of schools collecting the books they no longer needed. In the first year 40,000 books were donated to us and it was insane to see how much decent stuff UK schools wanted to give away. We then spent weeks sorting the books to ensure their relevance and boxing them up for shipment, which was to be paid for by our group fundraising efforts. Oh how our friends grew to love TBP's constant pleas for cash.

Spending that summer of 2005 in Tanzania was when it all came together for me. Six of us (Rachel and Nikki included) distributed the books we'd collected to schools in a region called Singida. As total novices to development work, our approach was a little haphazard and ill-thought through. Even so, the impact was still remarkable. The schools we visited shared one textbook between ten; most only had enough books to fill a single shelf. We were welcomed with open arms by teachers and students alike, all eager to have more resources to help them learn and thrilled to receive the subject-specific sets of books we'd brought. This made me feel good of course and by the time we'd climbed Mount Kilimanjaro and spent a few days sunning ourselves on Zanzibar, I was sold. There was no way we were going to let this go. So, together with Rachel and Nikki, we returned to university determined to add another priority to that of writing our final year dissertations – to make TBP massive.

We registered as a charity and renamed ourselves READ International (www.readinternational.org.uk) – a grand enough name, we hoped, to con people into thinking we were bigger than we really were. READ had become my personal mission and as soon as our final term was over, I took it on full-time and grew the network of universities and students involved. With Nikki, Rachel and Tom as our first trustees, I set up READ HQ at my dad's kitchen table and lived off his generosity for over a year.

Until March 2011, READ was my life and by default it was Nikki's, too.

In 2007, READ International won 'Best New Charity' in the Charity Times Awards and we were recognised as the 'Best International Aid and Development Charity' in 2010. In 2011, we sent our one millionth book to East Africa, and had not only impacted over 500,000 African students but had worked with well over 1000 student volunteers at over 50 universities across the UK. None of this would have been possible, of course, without the support of a truly exceptional and loyal team of staff and student interns. I certainly don't claim these achievements as all my own doing.

In time we decided to collect books from anyone and not just educational books. We now even have book collection bins on the streets of London. We have developed an electronic book sorting system so we just scan the barcode on a book and it will tell us how relevant it is for an East African curriculum. Any books not relevant we sell through a partnership with an online retail social enterprise, Better World Books, to generate revenue to fund our operations. We have expanded to give development training to our student volunteers; teach global citizenship in UK schools; and train our recipient teachers in East Africa on how best to manage their books. We also now work in collaboration with recipient school students to help them build and refurbish their libraries so as to foster a reading culture and create a sense of ownership and pride in their new facilities.

The team and I got a real buzz out of harnessing any excess capacity in the private sector and developed corporate partnerships to keep our operating costs down. KPMG gave free office space in East Africa, DHL gave free logistical support, Big Yellow Storage stored all our books for free across the UK, British Airways gave free flights to our staff, Staples donated free stationery and the British Library supported our work. The list doesn't even cover them all – testimony to the generosity of many corporations and our unfailing determination to get stuff for free.

However, despite all this success and exciting achievements, I decided to move on from READ in 2011. I wanted new leadership to introduce differing perspectives to the organisation's work. Not only was I becoming ever more paranoid about the dreaded 'founder's syndrome' but I was ready to take on a new challenge myself. Within two days of leaving READ, Nikki and I were on an aeroplane starting our *On the Up* adventure – a shared dream which we'd been shaping for several years.

We'll save the tales of our journey for the chapters to come but right now we're back on UK soil where I find myself immersed in the social entrepreneurship scene. I'm currently working at Ashoka (www. ashoka.org), with a specific job to support students to consider their potential role in driving social change. I'm also further developing two other social enterprises I have co-founded: NoPC (www.nopc.org.uk), a cloud-based solution bringing computing, educational software and internet access to remote locations; and Wripped (www.wripped.org), a disruptive publishing enterprise. Both are based on learning from my experience at READ and a desire to turn business thinking to development challenges. I have no clue about exactly what the future holds (Nikki's the one with the life plan). I just know how lucky I've been and hope that the years to come will include some more of the same.

About Nikki (by Nikki)

As you can see from Rob's introduction, much of our charitable experience at university was shared. I won't bore you with the same stories but there are one or two bits I'll add, starting with my own gap year experience. My grandfather had been posted to India during World War II and he spent most of my childhood telling me tales about this 'far flung place' where people speak English with a funny accent and worship gods with many heads. From the moment I learnt about the concept of taking a gap year, I set my heart on retracing his steps and experiencing the madness of India for myself.

Instead of just travelling, the plan was to be a little more earnest with my time and spend six months working in an orphanage. Everything was in place, the romantic vision almost a reality. Then India and Pakistan started threatening nuclear Armageddon and I was told that British Nationals shouldn't travel to the area. Gutted. My gap year company sent me a list of new options and I formulated a 'Plan B': six months teaching English in a Chinese city I'd never heard of. Despite not being my first choice, my experience in China was akin to Rob's epiphany in Tanzania and it was this which made me promise myself that I'd never settle for a 'normal job' (whatever that is anyway).

My gap year was, of course, as much about my own enjoyment and personal development as it was about teaching Chinese kids how to sing 'Merry Christmas' in English. Similar to Rob, I too spent my first real overseas adventure drinking copious volumes of Chinese beer, becoming totally caught up in a new culture and visiting some of the world's most mind-blowing sights. That said there was something all the more rewarding about teaching impressionable kids a language that many of them were desperate to learn. For them it was a way to open up their opportunities and a potential ticket to the western world.

I so clearly remember the moment when Rob told me that volunteering projects were a complete waste of time. I gave him the Nikki 'special death stare' and took umbrage at his painfully laddish tone. However, if dismissing the richness of the volunteering experience had offended me, I was convinced that Rob could be converted to my point of view. Did I ever imagine that he would become 'Mr Volunteering'? I did not. However, the founding, and subsequent success, of READ International vindicated my quiet campaign to make Rob a more charitable man!

When it came to finding a job at the end of university, I knew I wanted to work in the third sector but had no real idea where to start or whether it would be possible. Until then I hadn't realised that you can work for a charity *and* get paid. Keen to gain solid training and new skills, I applied for the graduate training programme at Cancer Research UK, and then had to go through the five gruelling stages of the application process. To my great surprise, I was accepted and I spent the next five years working for the charity in a range of highly varied fundraising roles, from Strategy Planning to Community Fundraising, Direct Marketing and Retail.

In the process I gained an incredible insight into why Cancer Research UK is the UK's largest charity and raises over £400m from the general public every year. Early on in my experience, our Strategy Director gave a presentation on the UK Giving Market and our Top Ten Competitors. Like most people I didn't like to think of the third sector as competitive, but when you're playing with the big boys it most certainly is. Whilst I found the word 'competitors' shocking at first, I soon got over it. I grew fascinated by the charity's application of commercial principles to raising funds for social good and their strategies for building their brand into a household name.

Cancer Research UK clearly stood in stark contrast to READ International – massive versus miniscule when it comes to size – but each organisation was bringing different benefits to the table. Having had hands-on experience of both big and small sized organisations, I'm fascinated by the differing dynamics. Is it better to keep your mission simple, or to take on a broader set of goals? Manage a massive staff team, or a smaller group of people who all feel close to the cause? Collaborate with others working in your field, or compete with them for every pound?

I'm yet to figure out any one 'magic formula' and remain curious to explore all the variety of ways to drive positive social and environmental change. This, amongst other reasons, is why our *On the Up* journey has been so interesting – giving us a thorough induction into the ever-evolving role of social entrepreneurship and the power which comes from individuals, groups, movements and organisations pushing for change at a grass roots level – which is, of course, where all charities begin.

I've never stopped placing value on volunteering, even though I now get paid to work in the charity sector. I'm a staunch ambassador of for the value of volunteering both to the volunteer her/himself and to society at large. It not only reconnects you to the needs of individuals and communities, but helps you to keep a grip on what really matters in your own life. Living in London, I find it worryingly easy to lose sight of those around you and let your work take over your life. I've therefore tried to make an effort to get involved with interesting local projects when I can.

Since coming back from Africa, I've decided to work for an organisation at the smaller end of the charity spectrum. I'm currently heading up the UK division of Wings for Life, a charity funding research into finding a cure for Spinal Cord Injury. Co-founded by the CEO of Red Bull, the charity's overheads are covered by the company, which makes us an interesting spin on more conventional Corporate Social Responsibility strategies. So for me, it's another cause to care about and a new model of fundraising to explore.

Rob's right though. I do have a vague life plan but I'm too superstitious to share it. Let's just say that I hope the years ahead allow us to continue having adventures – both on a personal and a professional level. In the meantime we're both hoping that we can somehow squeeze in another sabbatical. So bring on On the Up II and maybe even another book to share with you all.

Rob and Nikki at the end of their journey in front of the Pyramids, Cairo

Introduction

" Ever since applying for funding from the Winston Churchill Memorial Trust[1] in late 2010 we've been challenged about the reasons behind our On the Up journey and, more importantly, been forced to articulate what we're trying to achieve. That's the trouble with funders; they make you work for your money. To be honest, this was tough at first because On the Up was born out of a 'mish mash' of different priorities.

We'd made a pact at university to do a big trip together and both felt the time was right. Given our experience with READ International, Africa was an obvious destination and the iconic Cape Town to Cairo journey felt irresistible. What's more, we were curious as to whether the rest of Africa was as endearing as the Eastern countries we had grown to adore. We were also recently married so people were starting to press us with questions about buying houses and having babies. Must run now, we both concluded, before life gets too serious.

Another huge influence at this stage was the two 'learning journeys' Rob had already undertaken courtesy of funders who had backed him at READ. He had visited India and Japan's most inspirational social entrepreneurs and after the two trips his energy was so infectious that it had kept us both buzzing for weeks. Thereafter, we knew we wanted to learn more about social entrepreneurs across the world and find a way to share their stories so that others could feed off their energy too.

Collectively, these motivations morphed into a plan for an 8000 mile journey across 11 countries, visiting inspirational changemakers who are building a new name for Africa. In terms of what we're ultimately hoping to achieve, figuring this out has been an iterative process. The hours we spent on long distance buses gave us ample time to mull it all over and by the time we got to Cairo we'd polished our 'elevator pitch' into three key goals for On the Up...

1. Inspire others to make change - We want others to feel confident that they can play a part in fixing the things that are broken in our world and feel compelled to join the community of people dedicated to doing something about it. *We want to leave people inspired and energised to act.*

2. Showcase social entrepreneurship - We want to use our stories not only to illustrate what this somewhat ambiguous phrase means but also to showcase the way that social entrepreneurs bring innovative solutions to society's most pressing social and environment issues. *We want to show people what can be achieved.*

3. Demonstrate that Africa is 'on the up' - The total lack of drama we experienced on our trip challenges those who would label Africa a 'dark and dangerous' continent. On the Up is our effort to counterbalance the bad press that Africa often receives and show that, despite the challenges, there are a lot of good things to shout about. *We want to celebrate the progress that is being made.*

1. Inspire others to make change

When was the last time you were moved to tears by the sight of one stranger helping another? Sometimes there is no hiding place when we're confronted by deeply touching scenes. But if you had to put a finger on that feeling, how would you describe it? Uplifted, moved, touched, inspired...? If you were to ask the psychologist Jonathan Haidt (a professor at the University of Virginia) he would describe this emotion as 'elevation'. [2]

Whilst we were on our journey across Africa, we both read The Happiness Hypothesis (2006) by Jonathan Haidt. A marvellous discovery because he summarised for us the emotional response we hope to create in people reading this book. He defines elevation as that "warm, uplifting feeling that people experience when they see unexpected acts of human goodness, kindness, courage, or compassion. It makes a person want to help others and to become a better person himself or herself."[3]

He goes on to say, "Indeed, a hallmark of elevation is that, like disgust, it is contagious. When an elevation story is told well, it elevates those who hear it. Powerful moments of elevation, whether experienced first or second hand, sometimes seem to push a mental 'reset' button, wiping out feelings of cynicism and replacing them with feelings of hope, love, optimism, and a sense of moral inspiration."

Forgive us if this all sounds quite ideological and if phrases such as "a better person" appear a bit preachy, but we're sure you catch our drift. As students it was in fact the stories of other successful changemakers that helped us to carve out our careers. Two people in particular were hugely influential: Clive Stafford Smith, founder of the human rights organisation Reprieve[4] and Dame Mary Marsh, former CEO of the National Society for the Protection of Children (NSPCC). [5]

Clive and Mary came to talk at our university and shared their experiences. They were open about their challenges and honest about their impact. Both had changed the lives of others but in very different ways. For us these were 'elevation stories'. Before then, we were undecided about our post-university paths. Yet after those two talks we were both left feeling certain that we should pursue jobs with a third sector slant. We're not saying that after reading this book you're going to be convinced that a job working for a social cause is the right career for you – those are big decisions and they're not ours to make. What we *are* hoping is that these powerful profiles will leave you feeling inspired and interested in the possibility that *you too* could drive social change.

There's a lot in the world that isn't working right now and we believe that every one of us can play some part in fixing the things that are broken. Whilst we were travelling there were plenty of poignant news stories that highlighted the need for new ways of thinking. Arab nations started rising up against their leaders, riots reaped havoc across London, famine took a grip in the Horn of Africa, nuclear disaster shook Japan, the global markets continued to be in turmoil and the seven billionth child was born. Each of these events relates to issues and outcomes that most of us find overwhelming and on most days we feel the same, too. We feel like insignificant players, powerless to act. We point the finger at others, often the government, or sit back and resolve that sh*t just happens – as it always has.

Yet there are scores of people out there doing their bit to shape a different future. Most of us respond passively by donating cash – research from Pay Your Way[6] published in 2011 says that nine out of ten British people are donating to charity with an average donation level of £100 a year. When it comes to taking a more active role the numbers drop but there are still some promising trends to report. The UK Voluntary Workforce Almanac[7] reports that in 2010 there were

765,000 people employed in the UK voluntary sector, an increase of 40% since 2001. This means that the sector now employs around 2.7% of the UK workforce. Volunteering is also a regular activity for a good chunk of society – in 2010/11 25% of people in England participated in formal volunteering at least once a month.

These are encouraging figures, but when you look at the gargantuan dilemmas facing our planet – climate change, depletion of natural resources, sky high debt, crumbling communities, deaths from preventable disease – we need *more* people engaged in *active* change. If you think that conquering this stuff is impossible then just consider whether anyone ever imagined a century ago that a man would walk on the moon or that paper wouldn't be required to pass information between people? 'We were too busy' or 'It was too tough' just won't stack up as answers if generations to come are forced to ask why London disappeared under water and the supermarkets ran out of food.

We're not naïve. Writing this book brings risks; we want you to feel elated, not deflated; empowered, not discouraged. But we're feeling good about our chances. From Alexander McClean, a gap year student who now works on death row, to Simon and Jane Berry, a mum and dad duo who are working with Coca-Cola to distribute medical aid; from Sherif el Ghamrawy, an ex-engineer who runs the world's first eco-lodge, to Erik Hersman, a blogger who's built an online mapping tool used in crisis scenarios all around the globe, our stories are incredibly diverse. Whatever your interest area, age or take on life, we're sure you'll find a story which leaves you inspired and hopefully eager to act.

2. Showcase Social Entrepreneurship

There are so many people working to alleviate Africa's problems that we could have spent years researching, travelling and telling fascinating stories. As it stood our trip was restricted to four months, so we had to choose a lens to look through. Heavily influenced by our experience with READ, we decided not to focus on commonplace initiatives. We also avoided large non-governmental organisations (NGOs) such as the Red Cross[8] or government agencies like the Department for International Development (DFID). [9] Instead we chose to focus on lesser-known social entrepreneurs whose projects rarely gain the limelight.

We have huge respect for many organisations involved in international development, the vast majority of which quite clearly come to Africa with the right intentions. But when you travel across Africa there's a lot to leave you disillusioned. There are countless interventions which have been left half-finished or subsequently fallen into disrepair such as schools, sanitation schemes and water wells. We've also been saddened by the dependency culture which has emerged as a result of poorly-designed projects whereby communities have come to expect others to help them rather than being enabled to help themselves. Whilst we're conscious that it's easy for observers to make sweeping statements like these, we are reluctant to hide our underlying belief that much of the thinking behind how to achieve sustainable social and/or environmental change needs to be shaken up.

This is where we think social entrepreneurs come into play. Rob was classified as a 'social entrepreneur' for his work with READ but before then this title had never entered our vocabulary. Once it was on our radar, however, we started hearing all kinds of references to social entrepreneurs and social entrepreneurship. The more we learned the more fascinated we became by what this approach adds to the mix.

The term 'social entrepreneur' was arguably coined by Bill Drayton who founded the organisation Ashoka[10] in the 1980s. Since then Ashoka has established a movement of social entrepreneurs around the world. Now a bit of a fad with the business school cohort, the ambiguity surrounding the term has got some people obsessed with analysing its exact meaning. We don't want to get tied up in a debate over semantics but it's important to at least touch on our own definition.

Essentially we define social entrepreneurs as people who bring innovative solutions to society's most pressing social and environmental challenges. Not limited to using traditional business, charity or institutional structures, they use whatever means possible to achieve their vision. They find creative ways to fundraise and are often unafraid of profit-making schemes. They combine ambition, passion and persistence to drive wide scale change. Our journey included visits to social entrepreneurs who were, for example, seeking new solutions to:

- **Child abuse** – Before Betty Makoni brought Girls Clubs to Zimbabwe, the issue of the widespread abuse of girls was not being addressed. Betty found a way to empower girls to stand up to their abusers and take control of their lives.

- **Sanitation** – David Kuria has developed a radical, for-profit toilet business which is transforming people's access to good quality sanitation facilities across Kenya and improving their health as a result.

- **Unemployment** – For the first time ever in Egypt, Raghda El Ebrashi has engaged multinational companies in a groundbreaking strategy to train and employ young people from marginalised communities, tackling youth employment head on.

There is an extensive literature which expands upon our own working definition of the social entrepreneur[11] so we'll leave the academic analysis to other authors and focus on storytelling instead. We want to use inspirational stories to showcase social entrepreneurship in a way that dry definitions cannot. We will share the incredible ways in which social entrepreneurs are changing their communities and countries – many with a vision to change the world. And we hope to highlight their talents, be honest about their challenges and pass on their 'tricks of the trade'.

We found a great variety of social entrepreneurs across Africa, all going about their work in different ways. Our general principle for shortlisting them was: the more different, the better. We've got a Buddhist monk training rats to sniff out landmines, a rap star leading an army of 'peace soldiers', a set of students who accidently got involved in a civil war and an innovation guru who makes a mint out of social start-ups. This list says it all. For us, quirky is king.

Free from the bureaucracy of larger players like international charities or government agencies, On the Up's social entrepreneurs are capitalising on their greater freedom to respond quickly and work from the grass roots upwards to mobilise change. Their solutions are multifaceted, diverse and unique. Their projects are in varying stages of maturity and they cover many causes – health, the environment, education, gender inequality, human rights, agriculture and much more.

Many people have asked us how we discovered these amazing individuals spread across ten neighbouring countries. It says a lot that we didn't find it hard – social entrepreneurs are not a scarce commodity. We looked first to our own networks, and then to global organisations set up to invest in, connect and celebrate social entrepreneurs, the biggest three being Ashoka, the Schwab Foundation[12] and the Skoll Foundation. [13]

We hope that whilst reading the chapters ahead, our stories will bring to life what it means to be a social entrepreneur. We don't promise to take away all the ambiguity but at least you'll be able to see that this isn't an elite or privileged category of superhuman beings – they're just people who've put awesome ideas into action. In fact we couldn't really care less what you call them – changemakers, social innovators, movement makers – pick whatever term you like. What matters to us most is that you feel their energy and some of it rubs off on you too.

3. Demonstrate that Africa is On the Up

It's rather ridiculous to make sweeping statements about Africa when you think that it's a continent covering over thirty million square kilometres with just over one billion people living in 54 different countries. [14] Cape Town and Cairo are like two totally different worlds and many in North Africa don't even connect with the concept of being part of Africa – they see themselves as being part of the Middle East. And yet of the world's seven continents, Africa arguably has the most preconceptions attached to it.

If you believe everything you read in the papers or hear on the news, it's likely that the word 'Africa' conjures up one of a handful of images: malnourished children too weak to brush the flies away from their eyes, murderous pirates abducting innocent bystanders, or maybe corrupt politicians rigging election results. Do any of these sound familiar? The international media have a huge amount to answer for.

We're not denying that there are a lot of challenges facing Africa – conflict, famine and corruption are undeniable truths. Rob has experienced first-hand the rough side of life whilst working in Tanzania. In 2006 he had to have his appendix taken out and suffered considerable post-op pain without any morphine. In 2008 he was jumped by a couple of muggers. Despite their being armed with machetes, he only lost his shoes and wallet, luckily not his life.

However, every time we re-tell these stories, we feel a deep pang of guilt. They're certain to capture your attention but they don't represent our overall experience of Africa. In reality what we've observed is that for every dramatic traveller's tale or headline-grabbing crisis, there are a million and one great things to report. Initiatives of all shapes and sizes demonstrate that Africa is a continent filled with people dedicated to driving change.

When it comes to foreign aid, many of us see Africa as a continent which is propped up by money from the international community. Whilst the amount of aid going into each country varies, the Organisation for Economic Co-operation and Development (OECD) reports that assistance from international partners on average now accounts for 10% of a country's Gross National Income (GNI) – a figure which continues to decline. [15] In the five years before the financial crisis (2003-07), the International Monetary Fund (IMF) report that Africa grew faster than most other world regions, with more than 40% of its countries enjoying an average annual GDP growth rate of 5% or more. [16] And according to the McKinsey Global Institute, more and more countries are now regarded as attractive investment destinations including Botswana, Cape Verde, Ghana, Kenya, Mauritius, Mozambique, Namibia, Nigeria, Seychelles, South Africa, Tanzania, Uganda and Zambia. [17]

As Africa opens up to the world, the pressure on African countries for better accountability is rising. What's more, African citizens are themselves demanding that their own governments deliver more tangible signs of development. [18] 2011 saw huge steps forward in governance across Africa. Kenya and Niger both adopted new and improved constitutions, South Sudan held a peaceful referendum, Guinea held its first democratic elections and Tunisia, Libya and Egypt saw the fall of their autocratic regimes. The hope is now that new governing parties will improve stability, address corruption and increase the freedoms of their people.

Probably the most well-publicised targets for Africa are the Millennium Development Goals (MDGs)[19] which United Nations (UN) member states and international aid organisations have signed up to achieve by 2015. News reports have so far tended to highlight areas where progress is slow and as a result some of the incredible achievements have been buried. To pick out a few from the many:

- The infant mortality rate (IMR) – defined as the probability of dying between birth and age one and expressed as deaths per 1000 births – has declined across Africa. [20] In all ten of the countries we visited, there has been a significant reduction in infant deaths over the last ten years[21]. For example, in Uganda the IMR has decreased from 91.3 in 2001 to 62.47 in 2011. [22]

- There has been a continuing upward trend in the political participation of African women. In 2011 women held 18.5% of parliamentary positions across all African countries (up from 15% in 2010).[23] Women's representation in parliaments in Sub-Saharan Africa is now higher than in South Asia, the Arab states or Eastern Europe.

- The majority of African countries are on track to achieve the MDG of universal primary education by 2015.[24] In Tanzania, for example, the enrolment rate for primary education has risen from 59% in 2000 to 96% in 2006.[25]

Pulling out positive statistics in this way does over-simplify the challenges facing Africa. An economist might be keen to point out that whilst Africa has seen strong economic growth, there is yet to be a widespread improvement in job creation and poverty reduction across the continent.[26] A political commentator might be quick to tell you that, despite regular elections becoming institutionalised in the African political landscape, many election results are skewed by vote-buying, bribery and voter intimidation. A health expert might want to inform you that when you compare Uganda's infant mortality rate of 62.47 per 1000 to the UK's rate of 4.62[27], the challenges ahead are more than sizeable.

We acknowledge that the debates surrounding international development are complex. However, we seek to use stories instead of statistics to illustrate our point that Africa *is* 'on the up'. Whatever the numbers say, nothing can deny the fact that the people profiled in this book are living proof that Africa is a place of progress. So too is our own travel experience – we took 25 buses, two trains, three boats, and three flights to travel nearly 8000 miles and yet we had not one item stolen, we never broke down and we weren't threatened once. If Africa was the irredeemably dark and dangerous place that so many people make it out to be, then how was this possible?

Happy reading

We know that most of you will be picking up this book with your own agenda but by sharing our goals with you, you'll at least understand where we're coming from. Goals two and three are relatively easy for us to achieve compared to goal one, which requires you to put down our book and *do* something – a decision which is rightfully out of our control.

We can't make anyone do anything, but to maximise our chances of success we need to ask you a few favours before you start reading...

- Open your mind to the art of the possible and start out from a place focused on cans not cant's.

- If a story makes you tingle, then stop, listen and learn. This feeling is telling you something about what matters to you and it's a great indicator for where you're best placed to make a difference.

- Don't use our choice of the term social entrepreneur as a way to claim that these people are special and you're not. Everyone can be a changemaker.

- If a chapter leaves you inspired to get involved, then look up the web links at the end of the article or log onto our website and browse our list of helpful resources.

Hopefully the stories of the people we met on our journey which have had such a powerful effect on us, will work their magic on you too. If you have views and opinions you'd like to share as you're reading then please do. You can comment on the stories through our website or post messages on Facebook:

Website: **www.ontheup.org.uk**
Facebook: **www.faceboook.com/ontheupcapetocairo**

Let us know how you get on, but until then, happy reading. And just so you know, Wripped Publishing will donate 20% of all the profits from book sales of On the Up directly to the social entrepreneurs featured, so you're already doing a good thing.

The Route

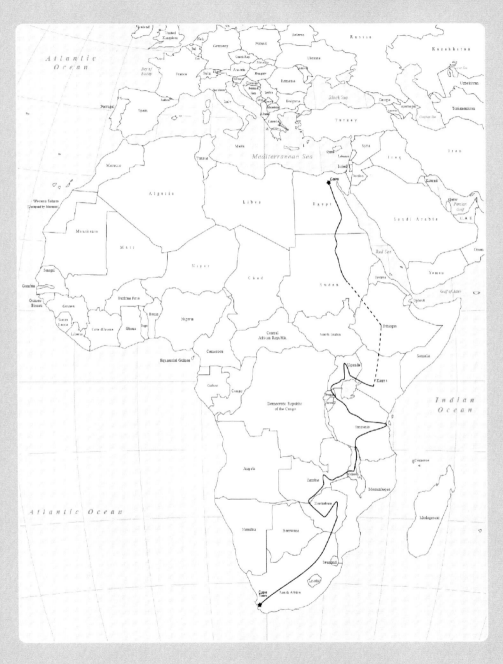

South Africa

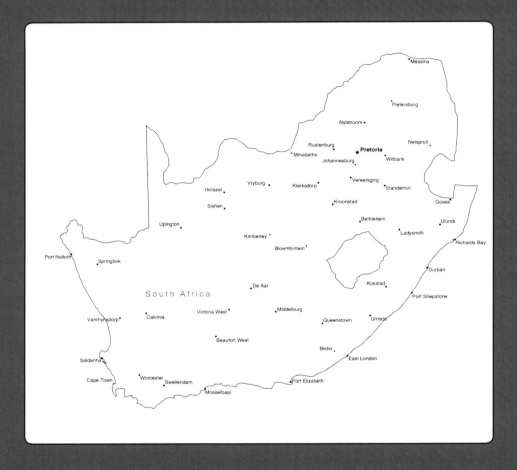

Capital Cities: Pretoria (administrative), Cape Town (legislative), Bloemfontein (Judicial)
Population: 48,810,427
Area: 1,219,090 sq km
Official Languages: Afrikaans, English, Northern Sotho, Swati, Tsonga, Tswana, Venda, Xhosa, Zulu
Gross Domestic Product (GDP): $554.6 billion
GDP Per capita: $11,000
IMF Poverty Index (of 190 countries): 71st

Key dates in history:

1652	In 1652 the Dutch established a refreshment station at the Cape of Good Hope, at what would become Cape Town on behalf of the Dutch East India Company.
1806	Great Britain took over the Cape of Good Hope area in 1806, to prevent it from falling under control of the French, which had invaded the Dutch Republic. The largely Dutch Boers fled inland in search of mineral and farming wealth and attempted to resist British influence.
1910	Eight years after the Second Boer War (1899-1902) the Union of South Africa, a dominion of the British Empire, was created on 31st May 1910 but the Statute of Westminster on 11th December 1931 paved the way for full independence.
1950s	Throughout the 1950s politically motivated racial segregation became collectively known as Apartheid.
1961	Independence from United Kingdom was gained on 31st May 1961.
1993	President F. W. de Klerk negotiated with Nelson Mandela in 1993 for a transition of policies and government and Mandela was released after 27 years in prison.

Charles Maisel

"F * * k that was innovative!"

Charles Maisel, founder of Innovation Shack

"NGOs are easy to set up and hard to kill off. That's the definition of a cockroach. You see so many of them doing the same old thing, it makes me want to vomit! God, would one of you think of a fresh approach for doing something?" Meet Charles Maisel. As controversial as he is kind hearted, this is one man whose view point shakes up conventional charity thinking.

The beginning of Charles's career looks like another great story of bright student done good. Charles's first endeavour after graduating was to set up the award-winning charity, *Men on the Side of the Road*, in 1999. The organisation, still going strong, provides men (and now women) who would otherwise be standing on the side of the road touting for work, with regular and suitable job opportunities across South Africa such as gardening, painting, taxi driving and maintenance work. A storming success, Men on the Side of the Road now provides 200,000 jobs per year, making a sizeable impact on the millions of unemployed.[28]

For Charles, however, becoming coined 'the guy who does unemployment' was boring. Aware of what works for him and, more importantly, what doesn't, he confesses that he hates managing people, can't sit in meetings and doesn't want to be 'the face' of an organisation. Charles's job criteria are simple: "I want to come up with new ideas, have fun and not work very much." Charles proves that you can live this boyish dream and still make money.

Entirely out of keeping with your archetypal charity worker, self-deprecating is about the last word we'd use to describe Charles. He's not modest about what he achieved at Men on the Side of the Road, winning world wide acclaim including a prestigious Ashoka Fellowship.[29] He believed then (and still does) that his creative genius deserved reward. Before leaving the organisation Charles wanted something in return that would allow him to live his dream of kicking off more groundbreaking initiatives. So in 2003 Charles requested a monthly royalty fee for having founded the charity. This 'founders fee', as he calls it, still hits his bank balance every month.

Eight years later, Charles is now receiving monthly payments from the plethora of other organisations he's since established under his company, *Innovation Shack*. As advocates of bringing business thinking into the third sector, we were surprised at how uncomfortable we found this concept. Searching for common ground, we felt a mixture of unease and awe when Charles said to us "I have no problem taking the money, no scruples at all." We inched down

CLOCKWISE:

Entrepreneurs at work at the Black Umbrellas Project

Planting up lavender cuttings

Just some of thousands of lavender cuttings collected

Many hands make light work

off our high horses when he told us that many of his subsequent projects have been businesses and not charities but we spent the rest of the interview flip-flopping between viewpoints – was this morally heinous or total genius?

Early on in our conversations with Charles he made it clear that he dislikes the label 'social entrepreneur', preferring instead the title of 'social artist'. Though possibly verging on pretentious, this description does gain traction when you look closer at his approach. Brought up in a family who ritualistically read the daily paper, Charles uses newspapers for creative inspiration. Every day he skims through multiple papers, looking at headlines, text, adverts and photos, never spending more than five minutes before picking up his next read. His mission throughout is to prompt spin-off thinking about how the problems exposed could be solved. He then sells his solutions, or 'paintings' as he likes to call them, for a cash return, just like artists the world over.

To give you an example, in January Charles was struck by an image of people protesting and carrying sticks. An ordinary reader might feel a twinge of fear, but an extraordinary reader like Charles began to think about how the traditional art of stick fighting could be commercialised. A quasi-sport, stick fighting has rules but it's fast and dangerous. Within weeks Charles had invested his own capital to set up stick-fighting tournaments in the Cape's townships. Before long they were drawing crowds of thousands of spectators, attracting coverage from the likes of CNN, the BBC, Al Jazeera, ABC and National Public Radio, and of course turning Charles a tidy profit.

As Charles explained more about the innovation technique he's perfected over the last ten years, he challenged us like a pair of his college students; "What's so good about newspapers?" We stumbled over our response and he was quick to explain that they're so powerful because "they're objective, accessible, current, diverse and world-reaching. They're like a daily snapshot of all the world's problems that need to be solved." When something strikes him, he jumps into overdrive. "I feel new things. If it's there I get goose bumps and my hair stands on end." With a backlog of 3000 ideas created in this way, he manages to put one idea into action every month. This officially makes Charles an ideas machine. But how does one person have the capacity to create so many brain waves?

Charles sees it as simple. You just need to look at everyday issues in a different light. He first struck on the power of this approach some years ago when he visited a client who owns a vineyard. Every year his client's business struggled with the same issue – when the grape growing season was over, his land lost money. Whilst Charles was mulling over the problem, he noticed the mass of fallen vine leaves which covered the ground. "Why don't you use those?" he asked. Until then, the leaves had been a hindrance not a help, another job for staff to deal with. But since that visit, the vine leaves have been used to produce *dolma* (a Greek dish of cooked vine leaves stuffed with a filling) and now his client turns a profit throughout all four seasons of the year.

This story is the reason why Charles calls his technique 'Seeing the Leaves'. His model is far from a kept secret and he doesn't want it to be: "I will always do my own stuff but I want to inspire people through my technique to come up with as many innovative ideas as possible." This is why he works as a lecturer at his local university in Cape Town and shares his techniques with students and corporates across the world. He has also recently written a book which is styled like a newspaper and explains his approach to innovation.

We were invited to one of Charles's classes and it was fascinating to observe. Whilst chewing gum, he made jokes and kept the atmosphere light. Reflecting their lecturer's relaxed approach, the students openly shared their latest innovations as they ploughed through the newspapers in pairs. Charles greeted each idea with a response that was honest but always supportive.

Just one month prior to our visit, Baden, a student from the run-down township called Lavender Hill, discussed an article with Charles about gangster crime in his local community. Baden, himself an ex-drug user, laughed when Charles asked him, "Is there any lavender in Lavender Hill?" When Charles suggested that they plant one million lavender plants in the township and sell them for profit to national retailers, Baden underestimated the sincerity of his eccentric lecturer.

However, after one email sent to his contacts, Charles was on the radio discussing this very idea – quickly garnering a response in which 200,000 cuttings were pledged and start-up funds donated. Three weeks later, the project was well underway and when we arrived at the primary school where the project has been set up, Baden was rushed off for an interview with CNN. Impressive. Charles stepped back into the shadows to ensure it was Baden who was the centre of attention. The project continues to attract attention and was recently featured at an exhibition for 'The Best in Cape Town Small Businesses' and they are on their way to getting their products into stores.

Charles's involvement in this lavender adventure is typical of his style. He tends to get involved in the start up phase of projects based on his ideas, offering guidance, contacts and often his own capital. Then he agrees his cut, usually just on a hand shake, and takes a back seat. He never takes shares, only monthly payments, as he wants to keep his level of ownership as low as possible. Blaming ownership for a lot of the world's major crises, he avoids owning anything. His house and business are in his wife's name and he joked with us that he thinks he only owns his car, boots and surf board. When Charles isn't spending his time pouring over a newspaper, he's usually found surfing, hiking or doting over his two boys.

Searching for what makes Charles tick, it became clear that he's more of an innovation addict than a social soldier. Whether it's got a social side or not, he admits that he lives off the excitement he instils in others when they stand back and say "f**k that was innovative!"

He also claims that he keeps his emotions well out of his work life. "I have no emotional involvement with anybody – not the staff or the communities," he said. This, however, we struggled to believe when seeing Charles in action. He brimmed over with pride about Baden at Lavender Hill and when he introduced us to Vuyisile Dyolotana, the 'Head Gardener' at the project, Charles's emotions were totally exposed. Vuyisile was the original 'man on the side of the road'; the guy who had inspired Charles to set up his first organisation and who's been a close friend and right-hand man ever since.

We also took a trip to *Black Umbrellas*, another of Charles's start-ups. Black Umbrellas was set up for black African entrepreneurs and provides work space

Lavender Hill Headquarters

Baden, Charles, Vuyisile & Marselle
working together on Lavender Hill

at affordable rates, as well as mentoring services. As we took a look around the office, everyone greeted Charles as 'Chief'. Charles had clearly taken time to get to know all the entrepreneurs at Black Umbrellas as, in response, he offered everyone personal encouragement about their business ventures. This was the final bullet in Charles's emotional armour. Charles might prefer others to think he has a carefree persona, but he clearly cares a lot.

A man who rules with a confusing mix of head and heart, we would defy anyone not to be fascinated by Charles Maisel. An economics graduate who refuses to vote, an ex-rugby player who collects art, an atheist who believe in Karma and an inventor who's made a mint. But not all of Charles's traits are quite this contradictory. One thing is for certain - he's a man of many ideas and not just one. After setting up Men on the Side of the Road, he could easily have clung to his power and become a Founding Director who refused to leave. But instead he went right to the other end of the spectrum.

During 2011 Charles set himself a mission to set up 12 businesses in 12 months, a goal which the Stick Fighting Tournament and the Lavender Hill project helped him to achieve. For most, this strategy may seem a little too manic. But whatever your viewpoint, the biggest lesson we took from Charles was this: if you're the kind of person who's great at dreaming up ideas, then don't get stuck within one organisation working on one solution; be brave enough to quit, buy yourself a stack of newspapers and let your next idea take hold.

For more info visit:

Charles Maisel's Blog: **www.12businesses.blogspot.com**
Seeing the Leaves: **www.scribd.com/doc/60031087/Seeing-the-Leaves-A-Newspaper-for-Social-Entrepreneurs**

Postscript:

Before going to print we were sadly informed that Baden passed away in January 2012 after being in a car accident in South Africa. The team at the Lavender Hill project have planted a lavender garden in his name and a bursary fund from sales of lavender products is currently being set up.

Shona McDonald

Stopping people in wheelchairs getting pushed around

‖‖‖

Shona McDonald, founder of Shonaquip

" In 1982, Shona McDonald's daughter Shelly was born with cerebral palsy. The doctor told Shona that the best thing to do was to put Shelly in a home and have another baby. But Shona vehemently disagreed. During the 28 years since then, Shona has been developing innovative solutions to improve the lives of people affected by disability. Far from a burden, Shelly has been Shona's guiding light and still plays an important role in her social business – *Shonaquip*.

As we sat drinking mugs of tea at Shona's large kitchen table, we were introduced to Shelly. Driving an electric wheelchair, she carefully positioned herself to be right at her mum's side and refused to do anything but smile. "This is Shelly," Shona said, "the reason all of this came about." When Shelly was born Shona refused point-blank to accept that Shelly should have anything other than a life just the same as her sisters. Through her own research and a bit of support from friends, Shona built a wheelchair for Shelly that far surpassed what the doctor had given her. "I just like making things!" Shona laughed and described how one of the mechanisms for this first chair was a windscreen wiper part from their old Land Rover.

Without any decent state provision, Shona was determined to create DIY solutions to help Shelly take control of her own life. She designed ways for Shelly to communicate using simple techniques such as putting pictures up on the fridge and on her wardrobe doors. Shelly would then stare at the picture of what she wanted to eat or the clothes she wanted to wear. And it was out of this – one mum's determination to help her own child – that Shona's mission grew.

In 1984, working with the therapists who helped to look after Shelly, Shona registered her first charity called *Interface*. Their purpose was to build alternative communications equipment for children who couldn't speak, an entirely new concept for South Africa at that time. Like all small organisations, they had to be incredibly resourceful. As a mum of three, this was a skill which Shona has perfected. "I'm very good at asking people to do things; a great case of someone who knows how to use my friends, and abuse them, too."

Leading the life of a privileged white South African during apartheid, Shona's work with Interface quickly exposed her to the plight of other families caring for disabled relatives; families she wasn't used to mixing with. "Through my

"It's about the user and th ervice not just the wheelch

million people worldwide require a wheelchair (W.

Incorrect prescription can limit users function and caus serious secondary complications:

CLOCKWISE:

Shona's homely office

Shona's hall way and stock cupboard

The range of mobility equipment provided by Shonaquip

Keeping the mission in focus

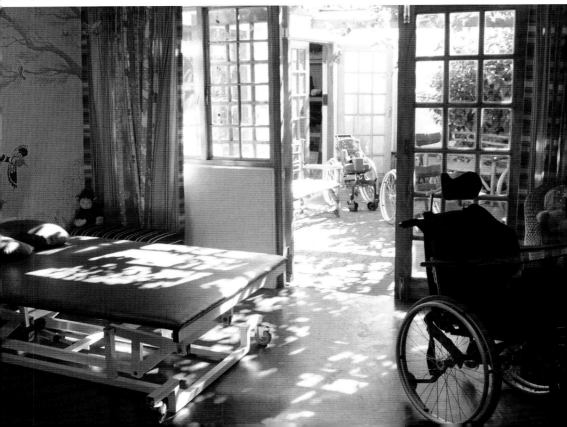

communications work I became exposed to all the other parents in desperate situations – hugely disempowered parents, especially in black communities who'd been brought up to do what the doctor said, simply because he wore a white coat."

The more Shona learnt, the more fired up she became. The stories were shocking and the stats were, too. For example, according to the World Health Organisation (WHO), an estimated 1% of the world's population, or just over 65 million people, need a wheelchair.[30] Despite still classifying herself as a 'home mum' at this point in her career, Shona's next venture was another new charity called *Empowerment Through Partnership Trust* (ETPT). This was an expansion of Interface and carried out work in a much broader range of areas including the provision of parent support, information resources and free equipment to families who couldn't afford it.

ETPT also ventured into the world of political lobbying where Shona learnt that any real change to the system would take time. During apartheid the white ruling parties saw little merit in equality and though they were primarily concerned with maintaining the racial divide, disability was still a huge taboo. ETPT pushed for a change in the segregated school system, trying to convince the government that education should be provided no matter the colour of a person's skin, their religion, language or *ability*. Thanks to Shona's growing reputation and the fact that she is white, her voice was heard. But the government was still not persuadable and the matter of disability in educational reform remained overlooked.

Although Shona was unable to sway the politicians, her own opinions had long been clear. ETPT's work was broad but there was one issue on which Shona became transfixed: the poor quality of basic provisions for all people living with disabilities – most critically, their chairs. "If you can't be mobile or sit upright then what's the chair for? It's just a convenience for the people who push you around," she told us with a mixture of passion and resentment.

Shona shared with us a story which explained her preoccupation with the wheelchair. During her time running ETPT, Shona was invited to run clinics in hospitals where she met a young boy who had been put through numerous rounds of surgery to try and correct his spinal deformities. After every operation he was placed back in the same basic wheelchair which was entirely inappropriate for his needs. Over the years this caused his whole body to mould itself into the same shape as the chair and, given his poor access to appropriate equipment, he eventually lost his life.

Ever since Shona built Shelly's first wheelchair, she has been tinkering with her wheelchair designs and supplying them to others through her start-up charities. Determined to address the issue of ineffectual wheelchairs on a much larger scale, and confident that her products were now tried and tested, Shona decided to morph one of the projects from ETPT into a for-profit social business known as Shonaquip. Operating out of Shona's home in Cape Town, Shonaquip sells modular disability equipment which can be tailored to an individual's needs and specially designed to tackle tough African terrain.

Before Shelly's birth took her life off at a tangent, Shona had been an artist and her eccentric home is a demonstration of her creativity. Step inside and you're greeted by rows of jam jars, giant photo montages, hand crafted sculptures and a pack of golden retrievers. In between all that, there is also an army of staff, every bit as warm as the homely environment they work in. Shonaquip employs 70 people, at least 30% of whom are disabled themselves.

Just around the corner from Shona's HQ there is a vibrant workshop where the wheelchairs are made. People in wheelchairs making wheelchairs. Why not? From here all the chairs are transported out to hospitals, schools and children's homes across South Africa, where Shonaquip's therapists then work with their clients and carers to, in Shona's words, "fit them, train them and maintain them."

Much more the average mum than the hard-nosed business woman, Shona remarked, "It was never a formal thing, we just did it. We just started finding ways to deliver on what we knew we needed to deliver on." For an 'informal thing' their impact isn't bad. Since its beginning in 1992, Shonaquip has become the service provider of choice for South Africa's Department of Health and has increased the number of chair types on the government tender list from four to 40. As a result Shonaquip conservatively estimates to have directly impacted over 65,000 lives.

To achieve this kind of impact, Shona has had to educate and encourage. She and her team have demonstrated their equipment to families, therapists and medical professionals, trying to make them aware of how much better life could be if they introduced a different seating solution for people with physical disabilities. And whenever they win people over, the transformation is quick to observe. As Shona herself explained, "We've been into centres where the kids are doing nothing but lying on mattresses and being baby sat by the staff. When we leave they are able to interact and are instantly seen by their carers in a totally different way."

Shonaquip has big plans for the future. Already working in Namibia, they want to grow their work to pan-African scale. But taking Shonaquip to these new heights requires new investment and a shakeup of their business model. In 1992 Shona decided to move Shonaquip towards a more pure business model because fundraising income was so unreliable. "I grew sick of being messed around by trust funds. They never wanted to support what you do for more than a year because then they'd think it was time to try something else and share the money out," she said with frustration. Interestingly, however, the purer business model comes with its difficulties too.

Shonaquip's success has opened up a market for competitors wanting a share of government money, the most threatening of which are the Chinese and Indian companies who sell their standard folding wheelchairs for a much lower cost. Though competition is a basic principle of market economics, the ethics involved in this scenario are tough. New providers market themselves as 'seating experts' but Shona doesn't think their products are built to last in rural conditions or designed to meet each individual's needs. Shona argues that: "Their costing structure makes them attractive contenders for ill-informed funders and short-sighted politicians but they are responsible for 'wheelchair graveyards' stacking up all over the world."[31]

Owing to their scrupulous reputation, Shonaquip are yet to be squeezed out the market but they're very honest about the challenges that lie ahead. Shona is closely following the ongoing debate surrounding 'impact investing'

A fleet of Shonaquip vehicles outside the workshop

Wheelchairs in production

whereby investors lend money to socially driven organisations, comfortable to sacrifice a higher return for a much greater social impact. Shonaquip would love to find an investor willing to help them grow their operation so they could achieve economies of scale and produce their equipment at a more competitive price, but Shona is sceptical about this ever happening, asking, "Who really wants to invest money in something if they're not going to make lots of money? Can they really console themselves with just knowing they have made a difference and be happy to get nothing more than their money back. That's philanthropy."

Despite running the business sustainably for over 20 years and believing that a business-focused approach is still the best way forward, Shona has had to compromise and go back to seeking donor funding for some of her activities. Previously, Shonaquip used the profits made from the disability equipment to fund policy, advocacy and research work, but now margins are so tight that this simply isn't feasible. Instead of scrapping these complementary activities, Shona has set up a separate charitable foundation to manage this aspect of their work which seeks funding from external sources and is topped up by finance from the core business. This approach, known as a 'hybrid non-profit venture'[32], is becoming increasingly popular across the third sector, and whilst it wouldn't have been Shona's first choice, it means she is able to keep the business afloat whilst continuing to sustain her not-for-profit activities.

As Shona's story teaches us, running a business with a social purpose creates all kinds of conflicting priorities. The rise of philanthrocapitalist funders like Bill & Melinda Gates can prompt people to think that business principles can be lifted and shifted into the world of social enterprise.[33] But we would argue that whatever way you look at it, it's a totally different rulebook. As Shona points out, "A social enterprise is about running a business for people, not for profit. Of course you still need the profit, but it's for the needs of the people first."

For more info visit:

Shonaquip: **www.shonaquip.co.za**

Trevor Field

"I can sell that!"

Trevor Field, founder of Roundabout Outdoor

"I can sell that," were the first words of Trevor Field when he struck eyes on an ingenious water pump solution which he now uses to bring fresh water to thousands of communities across Africa. Never more animated than when his pitter-patter is in full swing, Trevor is a thoroughbred salesman who has proven that a sales mentality can accelerate social change.

A born-Brummie with a thick South African twang, Trevor fondly recalls coming to South Africa in his "headbanger years" when he was concerned with little more than "having a bloody good time and earning damn good money." Building on his experience selling hi-fi's and washing machines as a teenager, Trevor picked up a job in South Africa selling advertising space and thirty years later, even though he's now a charity man, he still calls himself "an advertising boy".

Ever the die-hard lad, it's no surprise that Trevor's first revelation about the plight of water shortages in Africa came when on a boys' fishing trip to the bush. Trevor told us how, "in a car loaded with 300 beers and a loaf of bread," he and his mates drove past a windmill which pumped water into a concrete reservoir. Trevor was struck by the eight African women standing in line with their water containers waiting for the wind to blow. But it was on his way back from the bush, when the same eight women were still stood waiting there that he really got thinking.

Then, by absolute chance, a few weeks later Trevor met Ronny, a borehole driller with an innovative vision for changing the way that rural communities access water. The two met at a convention which Trevor was reluctantly dragged along to in order to keep his father-in-law amused. However, Ronny was there with a definite purpose, to showcase his 'Play Pump System' – an invention he had dreamt up after years of working on drilling projects in the bush.

The Play Pump does what it says on the tin. Kids razz around on a playground-style roundabout which doubles up as a pump, retrieving water from a 50 metre-deep borehole below them. The water then passes through a filtering system and flows into a giant container mounted on a tower. A hand-operated tap is plumbed in below the tower and, hey presto, the kids' energy gets converted into a free, clean water source for the whole community. To put in context how important this is, the United Nations estimate that 40% of people in Africa live in water-deprived areas.[34]

YES
TO LIFE!
SUPPORT
NELSON MANDELA'S
HIV AIDS CAMPAIGN

46664™
It's in our hands

CLOCKWISE:

A Playpump in action

Kids energy is converted into a free, clean water source for the community

Trevor talking us through the ways it works

HIV messages take up half the advertising space

When Trevor saw Ronny's mock up model of the Play Pump, he was infatuated by its brilliance. But he wasn't just excited by the idea of helping the women he'd seen stood waiting for the wind. Trevor's sales sensor pictured billboards on every water tower advertising Colgate, Vodacom, Sunlight Soap and other consumer products to communities who didn't yet have exposure to mass-marketing campaigns.

He persuaded Ronny to sell him the exclusive rights to the Play Pump solution and set about trying to prove his concept. He convinced the Government Department of Water Affairs to drill him a couple of holes and set up a two pump trial in Kwa Zulu Natal, a rural area eight hours drive out of Johannesburg. Although Trevor was willing to take whatever opportunity he could get, he chose this location because it had all the contributing factors for success: water was scarce but kids and potential consumers were not.

To his delight, Trevor proved that not only were the pumps hugely popular, but that advertising Sasco (a new brand of bread) on the tower billboard brought the sales figures of Blue Ribband (a competitor bread brand with no advertising) down by 78%. This gave him the confidence that he could attract enough advertising revenue to pay for the installation and maintenance of these life-saving water pumps, whilst hopefully turning a little profit on top.

So at the tender age of 45, Trevor took the leap. He quit his conventional lifestyle and set up a company called *Roundabout Outdoor* with a business partner. Together they quickly attracted serious interest. When they presented their business plan to a forward-thinking outdoor advertising agency, the agency offered to buy half the company, convinced that their own clients would snap up this opportunity to get access to new audiences. True to Trevor's original vision, the sale of advertising space on the water towers has been a success.

A bright yellow billboard advertising Sunlight Soap shone out like a beacon above the trees at the Play Pump we visited. However, when we tell you that the majority of Play Pumps are installed in school playgrounds, an ethical advertising debate kicks off. Like it or not, this is one of the most logical places for Play Pumps to be fitted; a place where kids and communities convene. Most of the advertising is not aimed at children but at their parents. However Trevor hasn't ruled out advertising products which appeal to a younger crowd. He candidly admitted, for example, that he would advertise Coca-Cola if only he could convince them to get involved.

Before you make your judgements, there's more to know about other areas of Roundabout Outdoor's approach. The organisation put concerted efforts into planning the best place for the pumps and work hand-in-hand with local communities to help them understand what's coming. Trevor is also very mindful about maintenance, something which some organisations building water pumps and wells fall down on. If a pump needs repair anyone can report the issue by following the simple instructions mounted on a sign next to the water tower. They just text the pump number to Roundabout Outdoor HQ who will in turn send out a local self-employed engineer to inspect the issue and make repairs. This not only means that pumps are kept in working order but helps to keep costs low by utilising local labour.

On top of the provision of safe drinking water, Trevor also gives away 50% of the advertising space on every tower to socially responsible messaging. As we approached another of Trevor's pumps, the HIV prevention signs were the very first thing we spotted. The ingenuity of this two-in-one solution (clean accessible water *and* relevant health messaging) has captured the interest of international donors ever since it was launched and Trevor has none other than Nelson Mandela to thank for that. Trevor tactically installed a Play Pump at a new school due to be opened by Mandela, and then used this as a magnificent PR opportunity. He rallied camera crews from around the world and secured himself 13 hours of international TV coverage.

Trevor had no idea that this PR drive would grab quite this much attention around the globe. Still a novice in the charity world, until then he had failed to grasp that if you have an awesome project, people will be willing to give you money for free. "People started sending money to pay for the things," Trevor told us with amusement. He let out a snort of laughter and added, "Nelson touched the pump and turned it to gold!"

With relative ease Play Pumps attracted the kind of funders most organisations would lose a leg for. And what's more, the funders came to him. He received a personal call from one US foundation offering him £500,000 and was offered an exclusive deal with One Water[35] (a UK-based social enterprise) where profits from their sales of bottled water would pay for more Play Pumps. With a never-say-never attitude, Trevor didn't even think to negotiate. "Give me some money and I'll do anything they like," he joked. Two pumps quickly multiplied into 200, which has since multiplied into 2000 across South Africa, Mozambique, Malawi, Swaziland, Lesotho and Zambia.

These donations have been crucial because Trevor's original business model, whereby the advertising revenue paid for all operating costs, has turned out to be unsustainable. This is partly because there are two disconnected demands at play – the need to provide a clean water supply and the need to sell desirable advertising space. When you map these two requirements on top of one another, the locations don't always marry up. Trevor maintained that providing water to those most in need was always the priority of Roundabout Outdoor and, as such, there are many pumps where advertising boards don't feature.

However, we did visit one pump which made us wonder whether the priorities always fall in this order. It was right next to a major cross road on a busy highway – clearly a prime location for advertising space but definitely not a place where communities would come to collect water. Trevor insisted this was a one-off, a pump they placed in the early days. Whatever way you look at it, income from this tower will pay for others in a more worthy location, but marrying business imperatives with social concerns is clearly not always a straightforward game.

Like most social enterprises with a commercial angle, Trevor has now set us his organisation following a hybrid model. He has a charity which receives donor funds and pays all the costs of installing the Play Pumps. Running alongside it, he has a Public Benefit Organisation[36] which looks after all the advertising revenue and ring fences some of the profits to pay for the ongoing maintenance of the pumps. Despite his operation being above board, Trevor still attracts controversy. A handful of international NGOs just can't get their heads around the Play Pump approach, claiming that the model promotes child labour and profiteering from poverty.

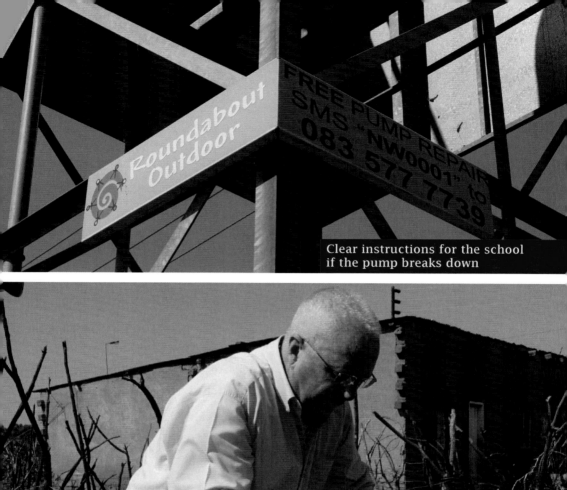

Clear instructions for the school if the pump breaks down

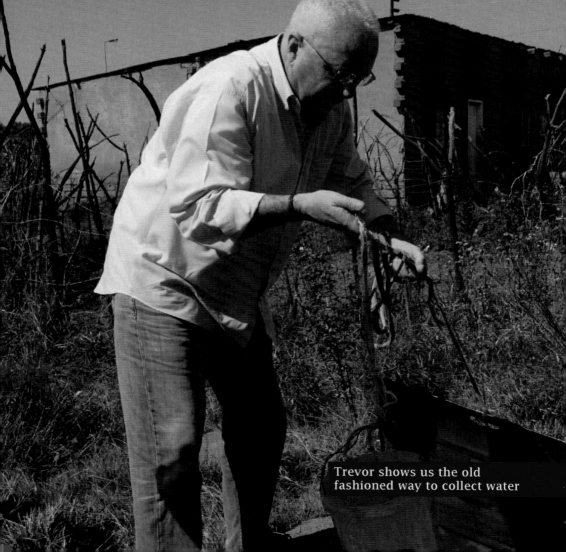

Trevor shows us the old fashioned way to collect water

But Trevor isn't phased by this criticism and nor were we. Play Pumps has achieved something that others in the sector should find enviable and it's no wonder that Trevor fought off 1500 contenders to win the prestigious World Bank Development Market Place Competition[37] in 2000. Many in the social sector find 'sales' a dirty word but Trevor's sales-focused philosophy is undoubtedly the key contributing factor in Play Pumps' unstoppable success. "They want us to go everywhere," Trevor told us.

After a day with Trevor we were left feeling pretty convinced that his love affair with selling advertising outweighed his passion for fighting global issues. But we were also left wondering whether it matters if the cause doesn't come first. For some people interested in charity work, their 'calling' isn't clear and there isn't an immediate cause which stands out. This might feel significant but believe us, it's not. Great skills, be it sales or something else, are always in demand and whilst it's important to be able to identify with your cause, too much emotion can be blinding. If you're able to be an objective voice in an emotionally charged sector, you're likely to bring clear cut thinking which might just save the day.

For more info visit:

Roundabout Outdoor: **www.roundabout.co.za** or **www.playpumps.co.za**

Zimbabwe

Kariba

Mhangura

Bindura

Chinhoyi

Harare

Victoria Falls

Chegutu

Marondera

Hwange

Kamativi

Zimbabwe

Kwekwe

Mutare

Shurugwi

Gweru

Masvingo

Bulawayo

Zvishavane

Chiredzi

Capital City: Harare
Population: 12,619,600
Area: 390,757 sq km
Official Languages: English, Shona, Sindebele
Gross Domestic Product (GDP): $5.916 billion
GDP Per capita: $500
IMF Poverty Index (of 190 countries): 160th

Key dates in history:

1880s In the 1880s, the British arrived with colonialist Cecil Rhodes's British South Africa Company to prevent Portuguese influence encroaching from the East.

1985 In 1895 the territory of Zambesia was renamed Rhodesia by foreign settlers in honour of Rhodes. What later became Zimbabwe was then Southern Rhodesia.

1923 Southern Rhodesia became a self-governing British colony in October 1923.

1953 In 1953, in the face of growing African nationalism, Britain consolidated the two colonies of Northern (now Zambia) and Southern Rhodesia with Nyasaland (now Malawi), a federation dominated by Southern Rhodesia. The union was dissolved in 1963.

1965 White political leader Ian Smith issued a unilateral declaration of independence from the United Kingdom on 11th November 1965 which was recognised internationally only by South Africa.

1980 Internationally recognised independence was only achieved after armed struggle in 1980 under Robert Mugabe who has ruled ever since.

Now Zimbabwe has been troubled by disputed election results, severe economic difficulties and hyper-inflation throughout the beginning of the 21st Century.

Betty Makoni, Photo ©Paolo Gianturco

Exiled for empowering the abused girls of Zimbabwe

Betty Makoni, founder of Girl Child Network

" **"Betty you know I love what you do, but just get up and go!" said a government sympathiser who admired Betty's work, "They are finding a way to get rid of you." After numerous arrests, this was the last warning for Betty Makoni from Mugabe's not-so-merry men. Her crime? Empowering a movement of girls across Zimbabwe to stand up for their rights and speak out against the injustice of abuse.**

At the time of our visit, we still hadn't met Betty, just spoken on the phone from her new home in Essex. This was enough to give us a flavour of Betty's character... tenacious, passionate and powerful. But the two days we spent with her organisation in Zimbabwe, *Girl Child Network (GCN)*, gave us a whole new sense of this formidable woman. To hundreds of thousands of Zimbabwean girls, Betty Makoni is an icon.

Like many social entrepreneurs, Betty has a personal motivation behind her work. Perfectly at ease with sharing her story, she told us, "When I was raped as a child, I knew I had been wronged and I also knew I wasn't the only one." She also grew up a witness to the cruelty of her father who regularly beat her mother. "I pleaded with my mother to report her suffering to a police officer but she said she couldn't do it. The family is our nucleus and we have to stay together – that is the mantra of our country."

When Betty was nine, her father raised his hand one too many times. For Betty's mum, this marked the end of her life. For Betty, this marked the beginning of her life's work. Resilient and defiant, she didn't repress her feelings, "My mother didn't have an opportunity to change her life; there was no platform to stand up and speak out. From this day, I knew I had to change things."

Against the odds, Betty successfully brought up her five siblings under the same roof as her father (he denied charges and was let off) and became a teacher at Zengeza Secondary School, Harare. Her first step towards changing things was setting up an informal club with a strict 'girls only' policy. Here, with Betty as their mentor, friends would discuss the abuses they were suffering at the hands of 'trusted' male teachers, fathers and brothers alike. In 1998, more than a decade on from her mum's death, a desperate young pupil confided in Betty that she'd been raped by her mother's boyfriend at knife point. Betty told us, "Her story was the final straw, it convinced me to quit my job to start a movement."

41

CLOCKWISE:

Nikki enjoying spending time with a Girl Empowerment Club

A Girl Empowerment Village at Chihota

One of many signs that cover each of the Girl Empowerment Villages

Every girl at the Empowerment Village is given a safe place to sleep

HERE ARE FIVE TYPES
OF ABUSES.

SEXUAL.

PHYSICAL.

EMOTIONAL.

NEGLECT.

ECONOMIC.

This one-of-a-kind revolutionary did just that. Since its inception Betty has grown a fledgling force of 300,000 empowered girls based in more than 700 'Girls' Clubs' across the country. Through story-telling, poetry, drama and singing, girls explore topics such as leadership, health, abuse, and most importantly, girls' rights. With this scale of achievement, Betty didn't need to be modest when she told us, "The real impact of my work has been changing the mindset of people. A girl child in Zimbabwe used to be non-existent, but now she exists."

But Betty's struggle to reach such heights should not be underestimated. Cultural practices which reinforce the repression of women are widespread in Zimbabwe. The Apostolic Church condones polygamy and marriage to minors, witch doctors prescribe a remedy of impregnating a young virgin to appease restless ancestral spirits, and having sex with an under-age virgin is commonly believed to be an effective cure for HIV.[38] As a result, many people have condemned Betty's work as counter-cultural. But this has never been enough to stop this force for liberation.

When we visited a Girls' Club at Chitungwiza School it moved us both to tears. After a morning of wincing at the harsh realities that many Zimbabwean girls face, our emotions on being surrounded by over 100 young girls singing their signature Girls' Club anthem engulfed us. If we could write this feeling into the dictionary definition of 'empowerment' we would. The words of their song translated as follows: "Abusers, we hold them in our palms, raise them above our heads and throw them on the ground!"

Thanks to GCN, the perpetrators of abuse are increasingly being held to account, but every day they still receive harrowing reports of abuse. When we met four-year old Chido, her story cut to the bone. Tentative about white strangers, she overcame her shyness and snuggled in to sit between us. The staff handed us a spreadsheet of case notes to illustrate the issues they're handling. Under the name Chido, it read: "Raped by her cousin at home. Case reported to the police. Trial date 03/05/2010." Needless to say, at the time of writing, Chido's abuser hadn't yet been charged and was still on the run.

When an abuse allegation like Chido's is reported, GCN goes to great lengths to support the girls and seek justice. But speaking out comes with serious consequences. Due to cultural stigma, girls brave enough to take their abuse cases through official proceedings are often no longer welcome in their villages. What's more, the whole case can all too easily be blown out if the local police officer is offered the going rate. In response to this, Betty has built four 'Empowerment Villages' to provide much needed shelter and support.

The first of these sits in Betty's homeland on the rugged eastern hills near the Mozambique border. With close family ties to the village chiefdom, Betty used her standing as a village 'princess' to openly discuss girls' rights with local leaders. With careful persuasion, Betty soon won them over. On land donated by the 'Top Chief', together they created the beautifully crafted Chitsotso Empowerment Village to shelter local abused girls. Now a village-owned initiative, the chiefs have also founded a Child Monitoring Committee (CMC) which oversees their zero tolerance approach to girls abused in the areas they govern. The same model is now used at all GCN Empowerment Villages.

Betty's work has created a mass following who hold her in highest regard. At the Chitsotso Empowerment Village they have adorned her old office with memorabilia including her old clothes, shoes and handbag. At every club, you can find, next to the obligatory mug shot of Mugabe, a mounted picture of Betty Makoni. Beyond her home soil, Betty has also won worldwide recognition including the CNN Heroes Award[39] for Defending the Powerless and an Ashoka Fellowship. It's no wonder, therefore, that a woman who inspires this kind of hero worship, was deemed a threat at a time when the government was facing waning support.

Betty described to us the event which led her to leave Zimbabwe in 2008: "I got involved in a high profile rape case with an 'untouchable abuser' that had serious repercussions. A financial supporter of Mugabe raped a 17-year-old girl at knife point. I was accused of being a liar working against Zanu PF. The government infiltrated my organisation. They came to my meetings and ransacked our office. A sympathiser within the government tipped me off to leave."

At the time of Betty's upheaval she had been at the helm of GCN for ten years. Already expanding the remit of GCN's horizons well beyond Zimbabwe, she had begun setting up sister projects which now cover South Africa, Sierra Leone, Tanzania, Senegal, Uganda, Ethiopia, Swaziland and Malawi. Under more normal circumstances, this could have been an ideal time for her to hand over her leadership to focus on her worldwide vision. But a number of factors have left the original GCN Zimbabwe in a far from ideal situation. Having their cornerstone wrenched away without warning left no time to wean them off their dependence on Betty. Although a new Executive Director has been appointed and Betty now sits on the Board of Trustees, it was obvious to us that the organisation is still struggling to come to terms with Betty's absence.

All that said, GCN has clung on and is holding it all together. But only just. Their funding model follows a more conventional NGO set-up and is reliant on donations from large NGOs, trusts and foundations. Though their clubs are relatively self-sustaining, they require funds to co-ordinate club activities, run their Empowerment Villages and cover head office costs. In their heyday, GCN attracted $800,000 of support from the likes of Oxfam[40] and other large international trusts. During the 2008/09 crisis, when political instability forced many international NGOs out of the country en masse[41], their funding plummeted. Only now are they rebuilding their financial support but it's far from what it once was.

It's hard not to judge funders who walk away when the going gets tough. You could also argue, however, that GCN should break their mould and develop a more sustainable source of funding. We're not suggesting that GCN should become a social business; it's impossible to see how you could ever monetise this cause. But there is definitely space to look more innovatively at new funding avenues so they can at least spread their risk beyond a reliance on trust and foundation income.

Meanwhile, since Betty has moved to the UK, she's had time to think about her strategy for improving sustainability and delivering expansion. She's registered Girl Child Network Worldwide as an umbrella organisation and created four different tiers for GCN projects:

Betty's old office where staff and friends have made a shrine from her belongings

GIRL CHILD NETWORK
MAUYA
CHITSOTSO GIRLS EMPOWERMENT VILLAGE
The Sky Is The Limit
THE GIRL CHILD NETWORK
MUZINDA WEVANASIKANA
ADDRESS PO BOX 253 RUSAPE
PHONE Nº 0912288251

The Girl Empowerment Project set up in Betty's home village

- **Tier 1:** These are fully operational projects with Girls' Clubs and Empowerment Villages. At present, this only includes GCN Zimbabwe but new projects will graduate to this stage.

- **Tiers 2:** These are independent projects working on girls' rights that have paid GCN for their consultancy advice and training. So far projects in Swaziland, Ghana and Ethiopia have used GCN's services in this way.

- **Tier 3:** These are partner projects that form part of the GCN Worldwide Network. They are replicating the GCN Zimbabwe model and aim to reach Tier 1 scale. There is now GCN South Africa, GCN Sierra Leone and GCN Uganda.

- **Tier 4:** These are partner projects in the western world that also form part of the GCN Worldwide Network. They raise awareness about girls' rights at a global level and raise funds to support the Africa-based GCN projects. The UK, Australia, Canada and USA all now have GCN groups.

This shift towards more strategic thinking will inevitably benefit GCN, and it's not just Betty driving the expansion. Tariro was the inaugural President of the first Girls' Club that Betty set up at Zengeza High School. With Betty as a mentor, she went on to gain sponsorship to study for a degree in the USA and then went to graduate school in the UK. Tariro then took a job with an American NGO in Uganda and instantly saw an opportunity for GCN's services. So she founded GCN Uganda, where she is now Country Director. Tariro is just one example of lasting change that Betty is making in developing female leaders across Africa. For every story like Tariro's, there are thousands more being written by young women leading more subtle shifts in their villages and homes.

Betty taught us some important lessons about how best to lead a movement which achieves this kind of change. Betty shared her own experiences of abuse with everyone regardless of whether they wanted to listen. She recognised the power of children to act as catalysts for change and taught young girls that when many voices come together, the fear of speaking out can be overcome. A role model and beacon of hope, Betty wasn't afraid to go against the grain and suffer isolation as a result. Despite her exile, she still has an unwavering dream for the future: "I want to fill up the whole world with our girls."

For more info please visit:

GCN Worldwide: **www.girlchildnetworkworldwide.org**
GCN Zimbabwe: **www.gcnzimbabwe.org**
Betty Makoni: **www.muzvarebettymakoni.org**

The names of all case studies in the story have been changed to protect the identity of the girls affected by abuse.

Marianne Knuth

Much more than a backyard social experiment

Marianne Knuth, founder of Kufunda Village

❝ Kufunda Village sits on a rocky plot of family farmland just outside Harare, Zimbabwe's bustling capital city. It could easily be mistaken for a collection of African mud huts, but look a little closer and you'll see something out of the ordinary... a community of Zimbabweans brewing up herbal tinctures, growing organic veggies off arid land and planting trees in compost toilets. The brainchild of Marianne Knuth, Kufunda Village is a living demonstration of self-reliance. Together the community is learning how, instead of relying on others, they can rely on themselves.

Before we take you to Kufunda, we want to share with you Marianne's past. Half Zimbabwean, half Danish, Marianne grew up in two colliding worlds. Not one to ignore difficult questions, from a young age she struggled to accept the supposed superiority of western ways. Marianne remembers her Danish grandmother as being very unhappy, whilst her Zimbabwean counterpart was every bit your life and soul. And yet they conformed to all the stereotypes. Her Danish grandmother was "beautiful, bridge-playing and relatively wealthy", whilst her Zimbabwean grandmother was, "very rural, strong and materially poor".

Marianne's pre-occupation with the global North-South divide played a central part in the years to come. Whilst studying in Copenhagen, she became a mover and shaker behind the World Summit for Social Development and discovered a passion for bringing people together to discuss pressing global themes. With this agenda in mind, she won an election campaign to become first, Director, and then Global President at AIESEC International.[42] AIESEC is a student organisation with over 50,000 members recruited from business-orientated courses across the world. As a tri-lingual high-achiever studying for a masters in International Business and Finance, Marianne fitted the profile of President perfectly. Her approach, however, brought something quite different to the table.

Opinionated, extroverted, goal-driven and egotistical – these are common traits of student leaders. And then you have Marianne. Gentle and utterly sincere, Marianne doesn't force her views on you, quite the opposite. Her interest is not in preaching her manifesto, but in bringing people together to figure out things in their own way. She doesn't play the end game and believes that obsessing about outputs is damaging. "Start small, work with emergence, trust and listen", she told us. As a couple of over-planners always

TEAS

MORINGA
IMMUNE
BOOSTER
POWDERS

SALVES

SALTS

2011 Focus Areas

- Living demonstration centre for food production & processing
- Intergenerational projects
- In communities more
- Closer integration among projects & programs at Kufunda
- Moving toward a living wage ($350/month)

Deepen our capacity for collective leadership

CLOCKWISE:

Homemade herbs in the Kufunda Village kitchen

Children outside the Kufunda Village school

The Kufundees

A permaculture garden grow fresh produce in previously unusable soil

Strategic planning

PIONEERS OF KUFUNDA
MARIANNE
SIKHETHIWE
CAROLINE
OMEGA
KNOWLEDGE
TICHAONA
LAWRENCE
FIDELIS
SHANE
JAMES
VEDZERAI
DJ WYNE
DIONE
NHAMO
ESTHER
YVONNE
SONIA
SILAS
ELIAS
JOHN
BEV

chasing a result, this felt totally alien to us and stood in stark contrast to the other social entrepreneurs we've met. In an effort to mirror her open-mindedness however, we resisted dismissing her approach as wishy-washy and quickly became enthralled by the merits of "letting things unfold".

After graduating in 1998, Marianne set in stone her life's mantra of "follow your heart". She turned down a conventional job at Price Waterhouse Coopers (PWC) and co-founded the organisation Pioneers of Change. Backed by big hitters from the US, Pioneers of Change stuck two fingers up at the people who dismiss student idealism as naivety. Cheesy though it sounds, the organisation was founded on the principle of "keeping the stars in the eyes of young people" and its core principles were:

1. Be yourself.

2. Do what matters.

3. Start now.

4. Never stop asking questions.

5. Engage with others.

Capitalising on Marianne's natural talent for facilitation, as well as her and her co-founders' bulging international network, Pioneers of Change attracted a 1000-strong community of graduates. In local groups, as well as in large gatherings, Pioneers came together to discuss how they could create positive systemic change in the world, using examples from their own jobs as food for thought.

In keeping with Marianne's style, the organisation didn't obsess about outcomes, but she did share with us a few fascinating anecdotes. One group of Pioneers who did take jobs with PWC persuaded PWC's Culture Team to refresh their Business Values. Another group was part of starting an international network of Hubs which provide creative work space for social entrepreneurs.[43] Pioneers of Change also acted as a launch pad for many of Marianne's current joint ventures, including the 'The Art of Hosting' (a global community of people interested in facilitating group conversations that enable action for the common good) and 'Reos Partners' (a business which supports governments, business and civil society organisations working in complex social systems to create positive collective action).

After three years spearheading Pioneers of Change, Marianne's heart took her off on in a new direction. She invited a group of her globe-trotting friends to celebrate her 30th birthday in her grandparents' village in Zimbabwe. At the party, attended by 200 villagers, Marianne succeeded in sharing with her friends the joys of 'real Africa' but it also brought home to her arguably one of Africa's most deep rooted problems. In a farewell speech, the village chief pleaded for support from the foreign visitors. "Without people like you", he said, "what could we do?" Marianne recoiled in embarrassment at this comment. In a country with so much to offer, she felt desperately that people needed to stop looking outside for help and start looking inwards to their own communities.

Compelled by a feeling that she needed to "reconnect people with the wealth and wisdom in Zimbabwe", Marianne upped sticks and moved home to live on her parents' farm. Totally at ease with the unknown, Marianne admits that she had no idea how she was going to achieve her vision: "I didn't know what it looked like to create a healthy, vibrant, rural community, but I trusted that I had enough skills to bring people together so they could connect with the questions and figure it out for themselves."

Marianne travelled around Zimbabwe's villages and, using her empathetic charm, she facilitated gatherings of young people and community leaders to reflect on their own life stories. Using examples from around the world, she motivated them to think about the resources they could use to overcome their own challenges:

- Modern building materials too expensive? Eco-building and thatching lets you build a house from scratch using natural materials from the forest.

- Land too arid to turn a decent harvest? Permaculture techniques can transform a useless patch of land into a rich vegetable patch.

- Dilapidated toilets and poor sanitation? Compost toilets are easy to build and even better, once the pit is full of your waste it makes great fertilizer for fruit trees.

- Medicine too expensive and inaccessible? Herbs that are easy to grow in your backyard can act as excellent remedies for a range of medical conditions.

Instead of teaching people these new techniques via conventional 'chalk and talk', Marianne realised that she needed a space where people could put their thoughts into action. Kufunda, which is the Zimbabwean word for 'learning', was built on a plot of land on her family farm to do just that. A living demonstration of the art of what's possible, every component of the Kufunda Village has evolved out of people's ideas for a new way of life. Not really knowing what to expect from Kufunda, we were amazed at just how inspirational we found it. In each hand-crafted eco hut, we found another surprise. A health clinic, an internet room, an herbal remedy lab, a mushroom greenhouse and then a pre-school. Marianne too has been taken aback at the popularity of some of the solutions, the compost toilets in particular. "We thought people wouldn't want to plant a tree in their shit", she said laughing, "but they're fine with it and their trees are very happy."

Kufunda Village could be judged as a social experiment in someone's backyard – yet it's so much more than that. It's a totally new challenge to sceptics who think that environmentalism is little more than a hobby for the extreme lefties of the northern hemisphere. Moreover, it's a practical solution to the perceived 'hand-out' culture, which so often gives Africa a bad name. Over the last ten years, groups of local people selected by their village elders have been coming to Kufunda Village to learn and explore what self-reliance means for them. They spend anything from a week to a year at the village and then transition their learning into their home communities. They are supported through their journey by 'Kufundees', a team of Zimbabwean specialists who work at the village full-time sharing their skills in herbal medicine, organic gardening, environmental housing and much more. The Kufundees, who all originally came from surrounding villages, are total converts to their new way

The compost toilet

of life and Marianne is hugely proud of their achievements. When chatting to the team they told us, "Kufunda is the lifestyle we've chosen to live. It's not work."

In trying to put our finger on what makes Marianne so special, we concluded that her personality contains a great fusion of African *and* European traits. She knows how to do business but she doesn't mimic the mania of the corporate world. Operating on her own kind of 'Africa Time', she proves that you don't need to constantly rush ahead to get stuff done. She's let Kufunda Village naturally evolve over the last ten years and, sensing that they are now ready for bigger things, she's moved back in full-time to support their expansion. Once Marianne is satisfied with Kufunda, she'll probably follow her heart into another awesome project which brings people together to tackle tough questions head on.

These qualities, coupled with her CV of achievements, are almost certainly why she was awarded an Ashoka Fellowship and named 'Young Global Leader of the World Economic Forum' in 2009.[44] But what really trumped it for us was that, despite her quasi-hippy ways, Marianne doesn't take things too seriously. After dinner in her house, just up the road from Kufunda Village, we cracked open a bar of Lindt chocolate (not organic or fair trade) and a bottle of good red wine (almost certainly imported) and laughed together at the irony of it all. Eating and drinking home-grown organic produce might be Marianne's ideal but there are a few places where she's willing to make an exception.

For more info visit:

Kufunda Village: **www.kufunda.org**
Reos Partners: **www.reospartners.com**
Pioneers of Change: **www.pioneersofchange.net**

Zambia

Capital City: Lusaka
Population: 14,309,466
Area: 752,618 sq km
Official Languages: English
Gross Domestic Product (GDP): $21.93 billion
GDP Per capita: $1,600
IMF Poverty Index (of 190 countries): 141st

Key dates in history:

1855   David Livingstone is one of the earliest and most well-known of the early European explorers in Zambia. He had a vision of ending the slave trade through Christianity, Commerce and Civilisation. He was the first European to see the magnificent waterfall on the Zambezi River in 1855, naming them Victoria Falls after Queen Victoria.

1880s In the 1880s, the British arrived with colonialist Cecil Rhodes's British South Africa Company to prevent Portuguese influence encroaching from the East. What later became Zambia was known as Northern Rhodesia from the 1890s and was administered as a British protectorate from 1924.

1953   In 1953, in the face of growing Africa nationalism, Britain consolidated the two colonies of Northern and Southern Rhodesia (now Zimbabwe) with Nyasaland (now Malawi), a federation dominated by Southern Rhodesia.

1964   Gained independence from United Kingdom on 24th October 1964 and became known as the Republic of Zambia.

Simon and Jane Berry

Coca-Cola saves lives

Simon and Jane Berry, founders of ColaLife

❝❝ Just imagine if the line you found yourself humming after every Coca-Cola advert was no longer "Always the real thing" but "Always saving lives". Thanks to the work of Simon and Jane Berry, this strap line is not as farfetched as it might seem. Born out of an idea dreamt up over 25 years ago, *ColaLife* is delivering medical aid to rural communities in Zambia by utilising the excess space in Coca-Cola's crates.

Coca-Cola manages to reach every inch of the Earth and in Africa you can be sure to find a trusty bottle of the brown stuff, no matter how far you are from the nearest town. Whilst living in a remote region of Zambia in the 1980s, Simon and Jane Berry used to marvel at the might of the powerhouse brand. "There was a population density of two people per square kilometre. We had no post and no phone. And yet we could still get Coca-Cola", they said to us over a morning coffee.

Love Coca-Cola or loathe them, their domination is undeniable and many people, Simon and Jane included, see this as a huge opportunity for even greater things. But how could Coca-Cola actually help to save children's lives? Child mortality remains shockingly high across Africa. The highest rates of child mortality in the world are in Sub-Saharan Africa - where 1 in 8 children will die before age 5.[45] Parents of three themselves, Simon and Jane were disturbed to learn whilst living in Zambia that "1in 5 died before (the age of) five".[46] When their two year old son fell ill with diarrhoea, they found out first-hand how life-threatening a simple illness can be. Spurred on by this personal experience, they decided Coca-Cola should help.

Between them, Simon and Jane are always brewing up off-the-wall ideas. As Jane told us with a smile, "We both have silly ideas but Simon has sillier ideas than I do and tends to hold on to them." When in Zambia, Simon decided that Coca-Cola should use their distribution network to deliver treatments for childhood diseases to rural communities where medical care was scarce, but Coca-Cola was not. The initial plan was to persuade Coca-Cola to modify their crates, adding a pocket on the side to carry these medical supplies.

Whilst still living in Zambia, they made their first attempt to contact Coca-Cola. With limited communication tools to hand, they opted for a telex and unsurprisingly, failed to raise a response. Simon and Jane then moved back to the UK, spent the next decade running a social business called ruralnet|uk, and left the idea behind. Or at least that's what Jane thought! In reality Simon had spent the next ten years with the Coca-Cola dream rattling around in his head.

In 2008, Simon was watching a live text blog of a conference hosted by an innovation organisation, Business Call to Action.[47] A brainchild of Gordon Brown,

CLOCKWISE:

Health and safety in Africa!

Ten AidPods now fit snugly into the top of a Coca-Cola crate

Village retailers come into a local town to collect more Coca-Cola from the wholesalers

A regional wholesaler in Eastern Province, Zambia

the conference was organised to challenge multinationals to see how they could assist development in Africa. When Simon noticed that the CEO of Coca-Cola was in attendance, his ears pricked up. The live blog was open for comments so he took another punt with his latest spin on the Coca-Cola concept... "Why don't you take one bottle out of every ten in a crate and stick a container of medical aid into it?" he wrote. He waited patiently for a response from the CEO. Nothing.

By now aware that the "silly idea" wasn't going to rest, Jane insisted that Coca-Cola would never take one bottle out of every crate. Instead she suggested that they create small containers which would fit neatly in the excess space between the necks of the Coca-Cola bottles. This debate went on for several weeks but eventually Simon conceded that his wife was probably right (again). The idea of these containers, now coined 'AidPods', firmly re-ignited Simon's vision and he decided to set up a Facebook group called 'Let's talk to Coca-Cola about Saving the World's Children'. Attracting instantaneous interest, Web 2.0 proved its power and they quickly gathered a following of likeminded people.

Within a month of setting up the group, Simon made an all-important move on the BBC Radio 4 website. He wrote his plea to Coca-Cola on the listeners' forum and rallied everyone he knew to comment. As he had hoped, his story was picked up by a live radio show, the much loved PM Programme hosted by Eddie Mair.[48] In what went on to become a 'Highlight of the Year' for Radio 4, Eddie pulled out all the stops for this alternative feature. Eve Graham, the lead singer from the New Seekers who sang the original Coca-Cola jingle, was convinced to broadcast a re-make of the tune with a new set of lyrics:

I'd like to fix those Burmese homes
Give poverty the shove
Grow sustainable trees, give aid with ease
And show Africa some love

Chorus
I'd like to reach the world and bring
It perfect harmony
I'd like to reach its outstretched arms
But I need a company
Coca-Cola
We need them today
They're the real thing

And at long last this provoked a response from Salvatore Gabola, Global Director Stakeholder Relations at Coca-Cola:

"This is an extraordinarily interesting discussion. And it is one which goes to the heart of the key question of how we can make better use of the successes of business to serve the development needs of the world in general and of Africa in particular... Together I hope we can come up with the right solutions. And I am happy to have a chat on this subject with Simon in the near future."

"Finally", Simon thought, "we're in!" So he went back to his Facebook group and pledged that once they had 1000 members, he would pick up the phone to Coca-Cola. "That happened quite quickly", Simon said modestly. After years of being shunned, Simon was exceedingly chuffed to find that Salvatore Gabola was more than happy to hear from him.

In the three years since then Simon and Jane have quit their day jobs and spent their time building on this foot in the door. They have developed every aspect of their business plan – the design and contents of their AidPods, their key partners and distribution model and their fundraising strategy. They have justifiably rebranded their "silly idea" as a superb solution to the provision of accessible medical aid across Africa, and in 2009 they set up ColaLife, a social business-come-charity. To summarise their latest approach:

AidPod design & contents

In the latest mock-up we have seen, ten AidPods will now fit snuggly between the bottles in the average-sized Coca-Cola crate. To get here the design of these pods has gone through numerous iterations but Simon and Jane haven't worked on this alone. Their online community of followers has grown to over 15,000 and they've all been given the chance to shape, analyse and challenge every aspect of the ColaLife business model, including the design of the Aid-Pod. Whilst Jane admits that this level of transparency can be scary, this process of 'Open Innovation' is integral to the couple's approach.

Their virtual friends have also been a rich source of expertise. It was through the ColaLife online network that Simon and Jane were introduced to Prashant Yadav – Senior Research Fellow and Director of the Healthcare Research Initiative at the University of Michigan, and previously a Professor of Supply Chain Management at Massachusetts Institute of Technology (MIT). He worked closely with them to decide that treatments for diarrhoea should be their priority. A set of rehydration supplies, including oral salts and zinc tablets, has since been developed, all of which neatly fit inside the pod.

Key partners & distribution model

In what Simon and Jane fondly call an "unlikely alliance", they have orchestrated a partnership between Coca-Cola, SABMiller (second biggest brewer in the world and bottler for Coca-Cola in many parts of Africa), UNICEF and the Ministry of Health in Zambia.[49] Together, these partners are party to ColaLife's first trial which launched in Zambia in December 2011. Finally a trial is underway to test how AidPods, filled with essential treatments for diarrhoea, can be distributed to rural areas, using Coca-Cola's secondary distribution chain. A dream come true.

The end-to-end distribution model for their Zambia trial is leaps and bounds ahead of their very first idea. Coca-Cola outsources the bottling of their products to SABMiller (among others), who then sell on the bottles to local wholesalers. These wholesalers then sell their crates to retailers running small to medium sized local shops in rural villages. A vital element of the trial is that the AidPods will be sold at a price. Firstly, the wholesalers will pay a per unit price for them. They will sell them on to the local retailers for a small mark up, who will sell them to mothers and caregivers for another small mark up. The cost to the mother at the end will be equivalent to the cost of 1-2 eggs however during the trial vouchers will be given out so that the AidPods are subsidised. By using the last steps of the distribution chain it ensures that the most far flung places receive medical supplies. And by putting a value on the pods ColaLife hypothesise that this will increase the likelihood that AidPods will get to the end user.

Coca-Cola bottling plant and distribution centre

Fundraising Strategy

At the beginning of ColaLife, Simon and Jane raised the funds they needed through whatever means possible, including a sponsored bike ride across France. They then landed a small start-up grant from UnLtd (a UK organisation which funds social entrepreneurs) which tided them over for some time. But with a major trial now in its launch phase the investment required is almost $1million. Although the pods are sold at a price, Simon and Jane still require a subsidy of about $1 per pod to cover all the associated costs.

Just before going to print, we found out that Simon and Jane have secured the cash they need from five key donors including Johnson & Johnson[50] and the UK's Department for International Development in Zambia. They have also recently won a global Ashoka Changemakers[51] competition granting them $10,000 towards their trial. Though traditional funding streams are being used at this stage, plans are also being made to ensure greater sustainability in the long term. One idea is to use the AidPod design and create an ethical consumer product for high street sale. Using the BOSS principle (Buy One Subsidise Several), the revenue raised would cover the costs of AidPod distribution. You wouldn't think that the clinical looking container could be sexed up, but when Jane pulled out an animal print covered pod we instantly saw its place in the travel section at Boots.

If the Zambia trial works out, Simon and Jane's vision is to set up trials across the continent. Once the concept is proven, they want to hand it over to existing agencies to run with. But before all that can happen, a long list of unknowns lies ahead. Will local wholesalers in the business of selling drinks be willing to broaden their offering? Will mothers be willing to pay for healthcare products when they're accustomed to receiving medical aid for free? Will competitor products like mobile phone talk time take priority over medicines? The list goes on but Simon and Jane are trying to foresee these challenges and are looking to their community of supporters to help them come up with solutions to match.

When we visited SABMiller HQ in Zambia's capital, Lusaka, the Director of Corporate Affairs was candid about the challenges which might de-rail the trial. "People at SABMiller don't want to be meeting Simon every day", Chibamba Kanyama told us, freely admitting that Corporate Social Responsibility had to deliver something to them in return. Doubts aside, however, Chibamba was very excited about the potential and has placed ColaLife on their list of Corporate Social Responsibility (CSR) priorities for the next financial year. When we visited SABMiller's central distribution centre we too got to size up the potential scale of ColaLife's future.

Simon and Jane are not your typical mum and dad duo. They are innovators, risk-takers, online wizards and masters of the art of mass mobilisation. What makes them rare is that after all the blood, sweat and tears, they're not precious about owning the outcome. "We don't want to protect the idea. We want people to be able to pick it up and run with it. Others may do it better or use it for a different purpose but that's fine."

People tend to say that as we humans grow older we get more set in our ways, but Simon and Jane's open-mindedness proves that this isn't always the case. They will admit that turning their silly idea into a superb solution has relied on perseverance and plenty of luck, but they also credit the wisdom that a few more years of experience can bring. Twenty five years might seem like a long time to incubate an idea, but how many people do you know who've managed to convince multinational corporations to partner them in delivering this kind of social good?

For more info visit:

ColaLife visit: **www.colalife.org**

Peter Sinkamba

Playboy millionaire turned environmental activist

Peter Sinkamba, founder of Citizens for a Better Environment

66 'The Copper Belt', isn't much to look at. At the end of a burnt out corridor in a half empty office block, Peter Sinkamba's office is in keeping with its charmless surroundings. If someone told you there was an internationally-acclaimed NGO working inside, you'd laugh out loud. But this set-up epitomised our experience of Peter – as one unlikely scenario unfolded, another would follow.

Started by Peter in 1997, *Citizens for a Better Environment (CBE)* works to promote the social and environmental rights of local communities affected by the malpractice of multinational mining companies. As soon as you drive out of Kitwe, it's apparent why this work is so essential. Clogging up the horizon are twelve copper mines (and counting). Though the mines bring essential economic gains to Zambia, their adherence to a rigorous ethical code of conduct is thought by some to be questionable.

Before CBE, local citizens had no way of speaking out against the negative side effects of the mining industry. In order to win business during the push for privatisation, the government set lenient contracts for mining companies indemnifying them against the harmful effects of pollution. Consequently, intoxicating levels of chemicals began to contaminate local water supplies and infiltrate the air. The impact this had on the health and livelihoods of communities was ignored until Peter Sinkamba made it his business.

Peter was already a well-known character before he set up CBE. As Student President of Zambia Institute of Technology (now The Copper Belt University), Zambia's President had labelled him "a radical young man". In 1986 Peter led his peers in a boycott of lectures in protest against new laws which removed student subsidies. Unfortunately, the government didn't take kindly to this act of leadership. Peter told us that they expelled him from university and blacklisted him from ever working in the public sector.

This made finding a job quite difficult in Zambia's socialist dictatorship where most jobs were linked back to the government. He tried to get work at a bank and then in the army, but both times his past record caught him out. He resolved that entrepreneurship was his only option and that was how Peter really earned his name among the masses. He set up his own company exporting maize to the Congo and within five years of being expelled he was on his way to becoming a self-made millionaire. "I was a very rich man," Peter told us laughing, "not this poor man I am now!"

ROOM 66

CITIZENS FOR A BETTER
ENVIRONMENT
(C.B.E)

IN THE SUPREME COURT HOLDEN AT LUSAKA   APPEAL No. 22/2009

                                           SCZ 8 /20/2009

(CIVIL JURISDICTION)

BETWEEN:

PETER SINKAMBA   APPELLANT
(SUING ON BEHALF OF CITIZENS FOR A BETTER ENVIRONMENT)

And

KONKOLA COPPER MINES PLC   RESPONDENT

_____

RECORD OF APPEAL

_____

CLOCKWISE:

The Citizens for a Better Environment offices

Peter surrounded at his work by case reports

Peter's legal books line the shelves

Peter takes on some of the world's largest mining firms, and wins most of the time

Peter shared with us some tales about this time in his life. He told us how he had hired whole commuter trains to transport maize across the country and how he won over the Congolese blood barons. And then, as one or two more beers slipped down, he explained how, thanks to his flash cars and private planes, he earned his title of 'Playboy Millionaire'. Yet, much to everyone's amazement, this was the life he chose to give up so he could set up CBE.

At first we struggled to understand why Peter would abandon his business to become an advocate for people and planet. It was clear from the glint in Peter's eye when re-telling his playboy stories that he wasn't bored of having fun or sick of being filthy rich. But the deeper we dug the more it became obvious that Peter's first love isn't making money. A relentless activist, Peter is addicted to speaking out about under-represented issues which deeply affect his country and more importantly, his people.

Both at university and during the years that followed, Peter used politics as a platform to get his voice heard. He told us how he'd been "one of the big boys" in the struggle for multi-party democracy in 1990. In fact, whilst running his company, Peter also co-founded an opposition party which became one of three major contenders for leadership in the 1991 elections. As General Secretary of a leading opposition party, Peter was elected in 1993 to sit on the committee reviewing Zambia's constitution. Throughout all of their enquiries Peter was struck by the fact that nobody spoke about the impact that business has on the environment. However, living in Kitwe, Peter was all too aware of the adverse effects the mines were having on Zambian people. It wasn't unusual, especially in the rainy season, for people in the city to suffer an incessant cough owing to unsafe levels of sulphur dioxide in the air.

Peter tabled his concerns, but the committee was all talk and no trousers when it came to environmental issues. This, of course, fired Peter up even more. "I'm a lion, a Leo", he told us, "We like to take on challenges and we don't get scared." So, much to everyone's disbelief, he sold his business and invested his own resources in setting up CBE. Eager to be seen as a plausible advocate for the cause, he moved out of his supersized home in a posh part of Kitwe and bought a new residence right outside a mine. Peter admits that this was a "very big sacrifice" and that his wife wasn't best pleased, but 14 years down the line, his passion is unwavering.

CBE's approach is not 'anti-mining'. They merely want the industry to play by the rule book. They gather evidence from local communities about the negative effects of the mines and compare this against a long list of laws, standards and policies. If they find that a company or government agency is in breach of their responsibilities, they prepare a case and present it back to the parties concerned. Thanks to Peter's standing, it's rare that his complaints fall on deaf ears and, where possible, issues are resolved without calling upon the law. Peter's power, however, is far from limitless and harder measures often have to be deployed. "When they become stubborn, I take them to court", Peter told us with a huge grin.

Peter's shelves are crammed full of serious looking law books and he was quoting the names of official acts at us left, right and centre. "So when did you get your degree in law?" we asked him. Along came another extraordinary explanation. In the beginning, CBE used to hire lawyers to take on their cases but they found that the law firms were too easily bought off by the mining companies. So, without any kind of legal training, Peter took on the role of barrister and decided to represent himself in court. He takes on companies in his own name, working on behalf of the communities he's speaking out for.

Peter's strategy has led to a fair amount of outrage. "Suing the mines was unheard of", he told us with delight. Naturally, the government hasn't been welcoming of CBE's activities and the law community is always giving him a hard time, incredulous that anyone could have the audacity to practice without qualifications. Peter has finally quieted these complaints by capitalising on his political influence. Thanks to his amendments, the latest Mining & Minerals Development Act (2008) now states that his approach is totally kosher and, better still, it states that no costs will be awarded against him as long as he can prove he's acting in the public's interest.

The decision to go to court, however, isn't taken lightly by CBE. Since CBE started, eight cases have been raised, most of them taking years to come to a resolution. In 2009, CBE brought a successful lawsuit against a French cement company which had not been making statutory contributions into the Environmental Protection Fund.[52] The High Court ordered the company to pay $13.5million into the fund and cover the legal costs incurred by CBE. However the company appealed against this ruling and the case drags on – it is expected to be resolved in 2012.

Despite the challenge of drawn out court cases, CBE has made some groundbreaking achievements. Another high profile case involved CBE suing a Chinese and a South African mining firm for the joint mismanagement of waste that was affecting the local water supply. In response, the companies spent $300,000 re-laying a pipeline which safely disposed of the pollutant. An even bigger win came when CBE, in collaboration with a research group from Oxford University, exposed Anglo-American Corporation and the Zambian Government for breaching the Privatisation Act, the OECD Guidelines for Multinational Corporations and the UN Covenant on Economic and Social Cultural Rights.[53] Instead of moving through the courts, CBE raised complaints at the UN Human Rights Council in Geneva and the Department of Trade & Industry in the UK.[54] As a result Anglo-American agreed to forego some of the indemnities they had agreed to in their Zambian contract, reducing their tax breaks and increasing their responsibility for pollution. The Zambian government was also put under the spotlight and was forced to produce regular reports on their performance against the UN Convention.

CBE has also orchestrated the re-housing of a number of communities, one of which we went to visit. Sat outside the first of a row of well-finished houses, Community Leader Hilda Shiliya, greeted us warmly. She and 65 other families have been living on their new plot of land for three years now, sincerely grateful that they were able to escape their old village."When they blasted, the cracks in our houses became very big", Hilda explained to us. "It was so bad you couldn't even stay in the house. People were putting in sticks to support the roofs."

Before Peter stepped in, Hilda had been trying in vain to raise her community's concerns with both Mopani (the current mining company in the area) and the ZCCM (the government-owned company which previously owned and operated the mine).[55] Mopani refused any liability, blaming ZCCM, whilst ZCCM, reluctant to take full responsibility, agreed to provide tents for the

Hilda Shiliya and family in their newly built village

Peter and his right-hand man Jones sinking a few beers and sharing their stories

community to live in. When Hilda contacted CBE Peter was disgusted with these terms. Unable to make ZCCM budge, he called up his contacts at the World Bank. Within three days the World Bank had ordered that ZCCM use a pre-existing loan to cover the costs of re-housing for the whole community.

Compared to the influence of many environmental NGOs, CBE's power is quite remarkable. This is undoubtedly linked to Peter's reputation as an ex-maize tycoon and political front-runner, but CBE has, in its own right, earned itself an international reputation which means they can open doors. Thanks to Peter's work in an advisory capacity, he has built strong links with the World Bank, the United Nations, the African Development Bank Group[56] and many others who wield control and influence over African affairs. CBE has also been recognised by numerous international NGOs and Peter is an Ashoka Fellow.

As a result, CBE's opponents have slowly become allies, and both the government and mining companies now turn to CBE for support. "If there's a problem, we tell them and they listen", Peter told us. A prime example of this came when Peter told us that the night before he had called up his local mine to complain about the sulphur dioxide levels. No court cases necessary, they immediately closed down the operation for further investigation.

Peter Sinkamba's story warrants a whole book, if not a Hollywood movie. On top of CBE, he has completed a Masters, is writing up his PhD, has a wife, four kids and a new political plan on the horizon. His energy topped every other social entrepreneur we met and we'd dare anyone to try and replicate his routine. Every day he gets up at 2 am, studies until 6 am, goes to the CBE office for a full day's work and then heads to the squash club for a compulsory beer (or five). Peter has plenty of plans for the future, including supporting others to replicate the CBE model in neighbouring countries and maybe even morphing CBE into Africa's first Green Party. Wherever the future takes him, Peter Sinkamba is one to watch and we wouldn't be surprised if one day we're supporting his campaign: Peter for President.

For more info visit:

Citizens for a Better Environment: **www.cbezambia.org**

Tanzania

Capital Cities: Dodoma (administrative and legislative), Dar es Salaam (financial)
Population: 43,601,796
Area: 947,300 sq km
Official Languages: Swahili, English
Gross Domestic Product (GDP): $63.44 billion
GDP Per capita: $1,500
IMF Poverty Index (of 190 countries): 170th

Key dates in history:

Pre-history Tanzania is probably one of the oldest known inhabited areas on Earth; fossil remains of humans and pre-human hominids have been found dating back over two million years.

1000AD Travellers and merchants from the Persian Gulf and western India have visited since early in the first millennium AD. Islam was practised on the Swahili Coast as early as the eighth or ninth Century AD. Zanzibar was at one time the centre for the Arab slave trade.

Late C19th In the late 19th Century Germany conquered the regions that are now Tanzania (minus Zanzibar), Rwanda, and Burundi, and incorporated them into German East Africa.

WWI After World War I the whole region was handed over to the British, except for a small area in the northwest, which was ceded to Belgium and later became Rwanda and Burundi.

1961 Independence was granted to mainland Tanganyika from United Kingdom on 9th December 1961.

1963 After the Zanzibar Revolution overthrew the Arab rulers in 1963, the island merged with mainland Tanganyika to form the nation of Tanzania on 26th April 1964.

Bart Weetjens

Giant rats to the rescue

Bart Weetjens, founder of APOPO

" At the bottom of the Uluguru mountains in Tanzania, a team of African Giant Pouched Rats are being trained how to sniff out landmines. If your first thought is, like us, that blowing up rats can't be right, then panic not. These creatures, fondly known as 'HeroRATs', are not being sent on a suicide mission. They just sniff out the explosives and then we humans do the detonation job. Who ever knew rats were that clever?

Anti-Persoonsmijnen Ontmijnende Product Ontwikkeling, or APOPO for short, is Dutch for Anti-Personnel Landmines Detection Product Development. Originating in Belgium in 1997, APOPO grew out of research conducted by its founder, Bart Weetjens, who first discovered his love of rodents as a young boy. For his ninth birthday he was given a hamster, which he adored so much that he used to take it to school under his arm. When he discovered how easy they were to breed, he started selling the babies back to the pet shop in return for a nice packet of pocket money.

Sadly, we're not going to tell you that Bart went on to set up a rodent breeding empire or an international pet store chain. Like so many of us, he was persuaded to take a much more conventional career path. After gaining a first class degree in Product Design, Bart landed a great job designing everything from ski boots to high speed trains. Or at least everyone else thought it was great job. "I didn't really find my place in society", Bart explained. Far from being a city slicker, Bart had become a punk rocker with an active interest in Zen Buddhism. His rejection of consumer society made working in product design impossible, so he quit, signed on to receive unemployment benefit and dabbled at being an artist.

So where's the link with landmines? Well, during this period of drift Bart became captivated by the coverage of Princess Diana and her work on landmine clearance. When he shared his interest in this area with his old professor and student mentor, Mic Billet, he was encouraged to delve into it further. Living off nothing, but with the backing of Mic, Bart embarked on his own research. Focusing on Africa as his subject area, he did an analysis of the severity of the landmine problem and the technologies being deployed to solve it. He discovered that, in general, the techniques were costly, slow and heavily dependent on expertise.

Searching for a new solution, Bart's breakthrough came when he discovered a paper written by a Jewish American scientist who had trained gerbils to identify explosives for airport security purposes. Bringing together his extensive

CLOCKWISE:

The HeroRat truck takes the rats to their training ground

A trainer takes his HeroRat through its paces

The HeroRats enjoy getting re-wards for their efforts

A HeroRat detects an explosive device during training

landmine research with his childhood knowledge of rodents, he had the light bulb moment that would lead to the birth of APOPO. Rats could be trained to sniff out landmines! When he shared his thinking with two friends the general consensus was "That's a stupid idea, let's do it!" So they applied for a grant from Belgium's Development Corporation and to their delight gained a positive response.

With this support APOPO began to take shape and by 2000, five years on from their light bulb moment, they had proven their concept. At this point they decided to move out to Tanzania, keen to be working in the southern hemisphere where the issue of landmine clearance is greatest. Though a range of countries were considered, Tanzania was the most enthusiastic about the project and ticked the boxes in terms of its political stability. Subsequently APOPO was donated a plot of land by the Sokoine University of Agriculture (SUA) in Morogoro and within three years the staff team had grown to 30 people.

APOPO's landmine clearance solution is fascinating. African Giant Pouched Rats are bred at APOPO's training centre in Morogoro. At 4-6 weeks of age, they are familiarised with humans and their training begins. Over nine months the rats learn, through a process of positive reinforcement, to identify the presence of TNT (the explosive compound found in landmines). Then, once training is complete, the rats are the flown out to Mozambique to join the team at APOPO's flagship mine action programme. Tanzania is not a landmine affected country, but Mozambique is. There are estimated to be three million landmines in Mozambique[57] owing to two distinct phases of conflict – the war for independence and the civil war. This makes it the ninth most landmine-affected country in the world. APOPO is one of three demining organisations working in Mozambique, supporting the country to achieve its goal of becoming mine-free by 2014.[58] To date, the rats have cleared an incredible 2.8 million square metres of land, uncovering over 1800 landmines and many more small arms and ammunitions.

Once the rats touch down, they must first pass an official accreditation test with the National Institute of Demining, which is designed according to International Mine Action Standards.[59] Then, once initial ground preparation is complete, the rats are attached to bungee cords and they get to work. When they indicate the presence of a mine, the space around it is marked out and then a manual detonation team moves in. The reason they don't get blown up in the process is that is takes at least 5kg of pressure to set off a landmine and the rats only weigh in at 1.5kg (not small for a rat!).

As total novices to the process of demining, we knew this approach was innovative but we didn't know why. So we did our research and found out that more conventional demining organisations either send in a team of people with metal detectors or use dogs to sniff out the TNT. Bart, a staunch advocate of environmentally friendly technology, explained to us the beauty of it. "We're faster, more efficient, less costly and locally sourced", he said proudly. In APOPO's model, rats can cover 100 square metres in 20-30 minutes (this takes human de-miners a full working day). APOPO can clear the land at a cost of $1.50 per square metre (50 cents cheaper than the average of their competitors) and the rats are indigenous to sub-Saharan Africa, whereas often the dogs brought in are not. In addition, APOPO's rat training technique can be taught to locals, rather than relying on imported expertise.

Despite being somewhat apprehensive about spending the day alongside giant rats and explosives, Bart was one social entrepreneur we'd been longing to meet. His organisation epitomised the quirky kind of projects we were looking for and in terms of prizes, he's got the lot. Skoll, Ashoka, Schwab, the World Bank and the World Economic Forum have all recognised Bart's work, so it's not just us who think this project ticks all the boxes. Despite these accolades, Bart is tremendously modest. "You put the spotlight on me, but it's the whole team", he said to us many times.

Despite living in Tanzania where Buddhism is near-on non-existent, Bart still practices as a Buddhist Monk and encourages the whole team at APOPO to join him in meditation classes. Though he's married with kids, he follows Buddhism as a way of life and this gives him extra reserves of patience – an essential quality when you work in research. "It was a bit of a challenge at first because the rats just wouldn't detect these mines out here", Bart explained. Although these initial problems are now resolved, Bart and his colleagues have been continuously perfecting their rat training techniques through trial and error since they moved out to Tanzania 11 years ago.

Bart is also a big believer in the huge potential of rats, seeing them as capable of advancing humankind in a whole host of ways. Indeed, mine action isn't the only application of rat technology that APOPO is pursuing. Their second flagship project is the use of rats in the detection of Tuberculosis (TB). In 2005, Bart saw a World Health Organisation (WHO) report that declared tuberculosis an emergency in Africa – a response to data which showed that the annual number of new TB cases in most African countries had more than quadrupled since 1990.[60] According to WHO, an estimated 1.4 million people died from TB in 2010, with the highest number of deaths in the Africa region. The positive news is that the incidence rate is falling across the world but nine countries in Africa, including Tanzania, are considered still 'high-burden' by WHO.[61] So, working with his wife Maureen, Bart decided to put the rats to the test again – could they sniff out TB?

It turns out that yes, they can. What's more, they're not bad at it. In a process called second-line screening, suspected TB patients provide a sample of saliva which is assessed under the microscope at the hospital and then sent on to APOPO for a second opinion. It takes the rats seven minutes to sniff their way through forty samples (this volume takes lab technicians a whole day) and, to date, the rats have detected over 2300 cases of TB that had been missed by the hospital. Given that on average every TB patient infects 10-15 others in a year[62], this means the rats have prevented at least 20,000 people from contracting TB.

The TB detection programme is still in its research phase and though the results are seriously promising, the funding is proving tough to sustain. In a profession where rats are typically associated with disease, Bart explained to us that "It's more difficult to persuade the medical community of the benefit of rats." These are two of the greatest challenges facing APOPO. When it comes to landmines, fundraising is marginally easier and the rat solution is moving from being seen as alternative to much more mainstream. However, the industry is heavy with commercial competitors and, over the years Bart believes that landmine clearance has fallen down the list of priorities for international aid.

Rob with a new friend (Nikki didn't hold one long enough for a photo)

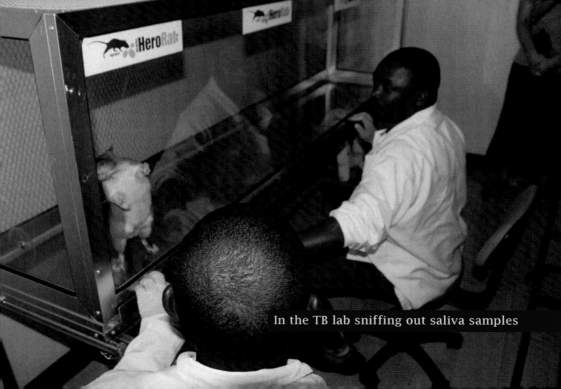

In the TB lab sniffing out saliva samples

Though Bart is open-minded about exploring the commercial viability behind APOPO's outputs, he's a big advocate of the NGO model. When it comes to landmines, he's convinced that becoming a company would compromise their high humanitarian standards and believes that "The NGO approach is the fairest way." Whether this hinders their growth remains to the seen. They are currently working on expanding their mine action efforts to the Thailand-Cambodia border, and have plans to take their solution worldwide.

Interestingly, as they grow their efforts, APOPO isn't planning on protecting their intellectual property. "We create science which is open source and accessible for anyone. As it's done with public funding, it's only right to open it up", Bart shared. Bart is not precious when it comes to sharing power with those inside and out of APOPO. He admitted that until a couple of years ago, no-one even had job titles (not necessarily a bad thing). Now that they're beginning to raise their heads above pure research and development, the team is starting to work more strategically and titles have been introduced. Taking a step away from the science, Bart is now focusing his time on the fundraising and business development conundrums which lie ahead for APOPO.

APOPO is one of those organisations where you have to see it to believe it. By the end of our day, we saw rats in a totally different light. Watching them trotting along behind their trainers, they seemed to rather enjoy their job. Given that they only work for 30 minutes every morning, leaving the rest of the day for playtime and sleep, we don't blame them! Bart believes that by challenging our perceptions of the resources we have around us, we can find answers to every problem on the planet. Given what he's achieved with animals commonly called vermin, we were left feeling that Bart is probably right.

For more info visit:

APOPO: **www.apopo.org**

Rakesh Rajani

Power to the people

869 ||||||||||||||||||||||||||||||||||||||||||||||||||||||||||||||||||||||||||||||||||||||||||||||||||||||||||||||||||||||||||||||||||||||||||||||||||||||||||||||

Rakesh Rajani, founder of Kuleana, HakiElimu and Twaweza

❝ "We don't think outside the box in the NGO sector, we just piggyback on what works", Rakesh told us. A Harvard research fellow, Rakesh Rajani is an intellectual mastermind who openly criticises commonplace approaches to development. "Lots of the official development stuff is crap, it's not working", he said candidly. Rakesh believes that real change comes when people stop looking to God, the government or the good-old international development community to solve all their problems, and start looking to themselves.

Rakesh Rajani is the co-founder of three high-achieving organisations – *Kuleana*, *HakiElimu* and *Twaweza*. Respectively sized at small, medium and massive, what all of these organisations have in common is a commitment to Rakesh's strategic 'theory of change'. He argues that when you engage people to take action on matters which mean something to them, you create a democratic force for change that concentrates the minds of the authorities on doing the right thing. To effectively engage people, however, you need public access to independent information and, more crucially, citizens who believe their voices will be heard.

Looking at Rakesh you might assume that he comes from the well-educated Tanzanian elite – he positively oozes intellect. Though Rakesh has received a first class education, his journey to the top has taken a somewhat alternative route. At age 13, inspired by a crush on a Norwegian girl, Rakesh applied to the International School in Moshi, Northern Tanzania.

When he visited the school he was in awe. "It was like magic," Rakesh said, "ten times more than anything I had ever seen." So he sat the entrance exam and weeks later received his acceptance letter. The yearly fees would cost one and a half times the entire family's annual income. His mother, herself a bright woman who had dreamt of being a lawyer, refused to accept the limitations and simply proclaimed "We will make it happen".

Harnessing their instinct for resourcefulness, the whole family devised ways to find the money. Rakesh gave us a charming list of their money-making schemes, the best of which really brought to life his entrepreneurial streak. During a national shortage of toilet paper (the only toilet paper factory in the country had broken down!), he collected up every spare roll in his home town of Mwanza in West Tanzania and sold it to the school in return for two and a half years of fees. And it was well worth it. Rakesh's schooling provided the platform for a degree in Literature and Philosophy in the USA, followed by a Masters and a research posting at Harvard. He cites this education, coupled with his mothers 'can do' attitude, as the two biggest influences on his career.

THE MAN-EATERS OF TSAVO

Strengthening Farmers' Organisations in Tanzania

CELEBRATING LITERACY IN THE RWENZORI REGION — AMOS MUBUNGA KAMBERE

Africa's Media — Francis B Nyamnjoh

Maral-Hanak — Language, discourse and participation

POOR ECONOMICS — ABHIJIT V. BANERJEE — ESTHER DUFLO

MONSON — Africa's Freedom Railway — INDIANA

COHEN/EASTERLY — WHAT WORKS IN DEVELOPMENT? — BROOKINGS

KOHLI — State-Directed Development — CAMBRIDGE

Impact Evaluation in Practice — Gertler • Martinez • Premand — Rawlings • Vermeersch

More Than Good Intentions — DEAN KARLAN AND JACOB APPEL — HOW A NEW ECONOMICS IS HELPING

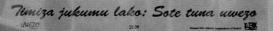

CLOCKWISE:

Every academic loves their books

Haki Elimu publications that Rakesh helped to produce

Some of the press cuttings of Rakesh and his work

A Twaweza poster

During his trips home from the United States, Rakesh became increasingly struck by the problems facing Mwanza, specifically the growing number of street children. Captivated by this injustice, in 1991 Rakesh put his academic pursuits to one side and returned home to explore the issue full-time. For Rakesh, working hands-on with children highlighted not only the power of their abilities, but also their total lack of rights. Always one to probe an issue further, he concluded that core institutions, in particular schools, were breeding a deep-rooted belief that children are inferior to adults. "Kids are silenced", Rakesh told us passionately. "If you go to school the most important lesson you learn is that to do well you have to be quiet, shrink, don't ask questions, never challenge and don't think outside the box."

It was this insight which drove Rakesh to co-found his first organisation, Kuleana. Starting out as a street children's charity, it gradually transformed into a child rights advocacy movement. Kuleana's advocacy campaigns covered issues relating to street children, child domestic workers, expulsion of pregnant school girls, corporal punishment, girl's rights, and education rights for all children. Their campaigns were implemented through numerous methods including workshops, training sessions, distribution of publications and media, and dialogue with communities. At its peak, Kuleana was awarded UNICEF's highest honour, the Maurice Pate Award, for its success in influencing children's rights issues in Tanzania. Although the organisation has now collapsed due to governance problems after the co-founders left, its legacy remains... Kuleana planted the seeds for Rakesh's second venture, HakiElimu, which set out to address one of the most fundamental rights of every child – education.

HakiElimu, undoubtedly the most influential of Rakesh's organisations so far, works to realise equity, quality, human rights and democracy in education by facilitating communities to transform schools. Founded in Tanzania in 2001, the organisation was born out of the frustration that education was not improving despite decades of well-meaning efforts, because, Rakesh argues, "people had been throwing technocratic solutions at political and institutional problems."

The Tanzanian government, like many governments around the world, has a habit of only reporting their own version of the truth. HakiElimu sees it as their job to respond to government conjecture about the state of education with objective information on rights, policies and performance. This information is compiled into accessible publications (usually short stories illustrated with cartoons) which are printed in the hundreds of thousands and distributed for free through their networks, increasing local impact and engagement.

More impactful, however, is the media messaging that HakiElimu put out through radio, television and print. In particular their TV adverts, which use funny sketches to challenge taboos, have proven hugely popular with the public. Thanks to Rakesh's passion, he was able to persuade Tanzania's media tycoons to provide space to HakiElimu at next to nothing cost. The adverts were so powerful that at times the TV stations were compelled by popular demand to continue airing them, despite the costs coming to several times above the contracted amount. If you search 'HakiElimu' on YouTube you can get a real sense of the ads – even though they are in Swahili!

According to the latest figures, the majority of African countries are on track to achieve the Millennium Development Goal (MDG) of universal primary education by 2015, with Burundi, Ethiopia, Ghana, Kenya, Mozambique and Tanzania having made notable progress.[63] This has been achieved through abolition of school fees, greater public investments and improved donor support.[64] This is a great example of progress in Africa which should be celebrated. However, organisations like HakiElimu are keen to see that this improvement is kept in context. Compared to increases in enrolment rates, there has been much less success in other areas such as the quality of education, completion rates, enrolment in secondary and tertiary education, basic education reform, and teacher recruitment.[65]

True to its mission, HakiElimu has got people speaking out about education. As a result of their work thousands of letters have been written to the editors of newspapers by citizens concerned about educational issues. If you ask anyone in Tanzania if they know of HakiElimu, they will usually say yes. Rakesh told us that a nationwide survey conducted in 2006 revealed that 79% of Tanzanians knew about the organisation and could cite their core messages - brand recognition rates that multinational organisations would die for. This can in part be attributed to the power of their Friends of Education Network, a 40,000 strong group of people across the country who are dedicated to furthering both citizen involvement in and the quality of education. In greater part, however, this level of recognition relates to the media furore surrounding HakiElimu during its early years.

One of the most significant and long running campaigns in HakiElimu's history was also very nearly its downfall. In 2001, with input from stakeholders including Rakesh, the Tanzanian government produced a landmark Education Development Plan for the expansion and improvement of primary education. Sadly, however, the vast budget allocated to this reform wasn't reaching the schools and even the most basic resources (books, tables, toilets) were still lacking. HakiElimu used their popular publications and mass media campaigns to expose the truth – that waste and in part corruption were causing money to go awry. What started out as a polite request from the Minister of Education for Rakesh to stop his work, soon escalated into a full-on battle. The government banned HakiElimu's materials and the President condemned their work in more than one public address. But the popular public support for HakiElimu was so strong that the issue became one of freedom of speech, and the might of the government was not able to shut down the organisation.

Events came to a head in 2005. The Minister of Education, with full support from the President, went to press claiming that HakiElimu was in breach of the nation's constitution. To the embarrassment of the Minister, however, HakiElimu discovered that he had quoted an outdated version of the constitution. The subsequent fallout, covered in the nation's media and wide public debate, left the government humiliated. A year later, with a new leadership in place in government, HakiElimu was able to negotiate a resolution through which every single restriction against it was removed.

What amazed us about this story was the enormous power an organisation can create when it has the people on its side. Over several months in 2005, HakiElimu was the second most covered topic in the newspapers after the elections. And this story was not the only example where HakiElimu calls the shots. Funding challenges have been an unsurprising theme across all of the projects we've profiled so far. So when Rakesh said to us that "Money is the last thing we worry about", we were fascinated. Rakesh's strategy is to go out to donors with the aim of creating "mutual deals discussed on equal terms". He's very firm about what

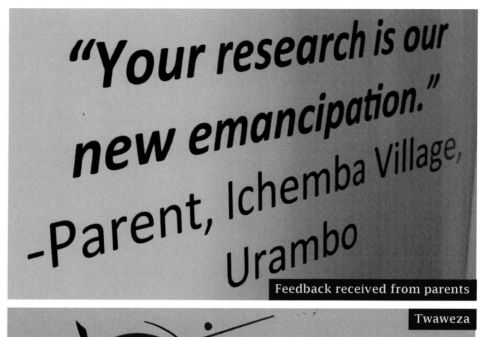

"Your research is our new emancipation."

-Parent, Ichemba Village, Urambo

Feedback received from parents

Twaweza

Twaweza

ni sisi

www.twaweza.org

he lays on the table and refuses to bend over backwards for donors with bespoke requirements.

In a challenge to all the organisations who struggle year on year to raise the funds they need, Rakesh discourages people from using a "begging bowl approach" and insists that "If you can't raise the money, you may need to look in the mirror". In the 20 years since he's been in the sector, Rakesh has raised millions of dollars and hasn't been afraid to play hard ball. At one point, the Department for International Development (DFID) wanted to fund HakiElimu's 2004-07 plan but in order to guarantee the money, the organisation was required to produce additional reporting – something Rakesh wasn't willing to compromise on. Six months later, according to Rakesh, DFID changed its rules and returned to HakiElimu, but this time the organisation said "thanks but no thanks" because it was already fully funded.

So how on earth do you get to a place when you can keep this much power in your court? Having a cause which resonates with the agenda of international donors has definitely helped Rakesh along the way, but the main reason he's been so successful is because his organisations have a reputation for hard work and great results. He communicates his impact with absolute clarity in a half year update, a comprehensive annual report and meticulously audited accounts.

Though Rakesh would have you think otherwise, he's also an eminent name in the world of citizen engagement. Having stepped down from the helm of HakiElimu in 2007, in 2008 Rakesh kicked off an even bigger initiative called Twaweza (meaning 'we can make it happen'). With $68m of funding from the likes of the Hewlett Foundation, the UK's Department for International Development (DFID) and the Swedish International Development Agency (SIDA)[66], Rakesh described the organisation to us as a "bold experiment".

Working across Tanzania, Kenya and Uganda, their goal is to broker partnerships across existing networks and communications channels (including religious communities, mass media and mobile phones) to provide millions of people with the information they need to drive change within their own communities. Using close monitoring, they aim to understand whether information delivered in this way actually leads to sustainable development, driven from the bottom up.

Through Twaweza, Rakesh is also engaging in a global effort to create more transparent, effective and and accountable governments. Working with progressive government and civil society leaders, Rakesh served as one of the more influential founding members of the Open Government Partnership (OGP)[67]. At the OGP's launch in 2011, Rakesh shared the podium with President Obama of USA and President Dilma Rousseff of Brazil, and delivered stirring remarks on the importance of open government, civil engagement and access to information. By the end of 2011, over fifty nations worldwide had joined the OGP, pledging to become more accountable and have their performance measured against rigorous benchmarks.

Whether working locally or globally, Twaweza represents Rakesh's belief in addressing issues at scale. "It's unconscionable to analyse a situation as affecting 40 million people and have a response that benefits only 400 or 40,000 people. That's a failure of the imagination", he declared. Rakesh also believes in looking at the root cause of an issue rather than putting a plaster over the outcomes. The more people we profiled for this book, the more we realised that there's a real spectrum of ways to address a problem; from tackling the source to treating the symptoms. Some, like Rakesh, have firm views that without the former, the latter is a waste of time.

Rakesh achieves a great balance of analysis and action. He's able to think big and deliver big, too. On paper he's a prime time candidate to be a CEO of a multinational conglomerate, but Africa is lucky that, thanks to his Tanzanian roots and his unfailing social conscience, he's chosen to work on the social advancement of his country and region instead. The greater the number of people who become armed with, and empowered by, the independent information he promotes, the greater the pace of change in Africa will become.

For more info visit:

HakiElimu: **www.hakielimu.org**
Twaweza: **www.twaweza.org**
Open Government Partnership: **www.opengovpartnership.org**

Rwanda

Capital City: Kigali
Population: 11,689,696
Area: 26,338 sq km
Official Languages: Kinyarwanda, French, English
Gross Domestic Product (GDP): $13.46 billion
GDP Per capita: $1,300
IMF Poverty Index (of 190 countries): 167th

Key dates in history:

1884 Germany was the first of the colonial powers to gain control in 1884 as part of the massive German East Africa. The Germans did not significantly alter the societal structure of the country. They favoured the Tutsis as the ruling class and aided the monarchy in putting down rebellions of Hutus who did not submit to Tutsi control.

1916 In 1916 Belgian forces defeated the Germans and took control of the territory. Belgium maintained the existing class system, promoting Tutsi supremacy and in 1935 introduced identity cards labelling each individual as either Tutsi, Hutu, or Twa. While it had previously been possible for particularly wealthy Hutus to become honorary Tutsis, the identity cards prevented any further movement between the classes.

WWII After World War II, two rival groups emerged in Rwanda, the Tutsi elite who favoured early independence under the existing system, and the Hutu emancipation movement which sought an end to "Tutsi feudalism". The Belgians dropped their long-standing support for the existing hierarchy by favouring the Hutu party.

1962 In 1962, the now pro-Hutu Belgians held a referendum and elections in which the country voted to abolish the monarchy. Rwanda was separated from Burundi and gained independence on 1st July 1962. Decades of high tension and many attack of and by both Tutsi's and Hutus ensued.

1994 The tinder box disastrously ignited on 6th April 1994 when a plane carrying the Rwandan President was shot down near Kigali Airport. Hutu's and Tutsi's blamed each other for the attack and it served as the catalyst for the Rwandan Genocide, which began within a few hours. Over the course of approximately 100 days, between 500,000 and 1,000,000 Tutsis and politically moderate Hutus were killed in well-planned attacks on the orders of the interim government. The international response to the Genocide was limited, with major powers reluctant to strengthen the already overstretched UN peacekeeping force.

1994 The Tutsi RPF restarted an offensive with support from Uganda, and took control of the country methodically. The RPF took control of the country by 18th July 1994 and managed relative peace ever since.

Mary K Blewitt OBE

"Pain, pain, grief, pain"

IIIIIIIIIIIIIIIIIIIIIIIIIIIIIIIIIIIIIIIIIIIIIIIIIIIIIIIIIIIIIIIIIIIIIIIIIIIIIIIIIIIIIIIIIIIIIIIIIIIIIIIIIIIIIIIIIIIIIIIIIIIIIIIIIIIIIIIIIIIIIIIIIIIIIIII

Mary Kayitesi Blewitt OBE, founder of Survivors Fund (SURF)

❝ **When Mary Kayitesi Blewitt OBE returned to Rwanda in 1994, weeks after the end of the genocide, she found out that 50 of her family members were dead. "How did it feel?" we asked her. "You can't explain to anyone. You just survive. You live. You exist. You're there but there's no words for it", was her reply. Despite the enormity of her loss, Mary** was able to look beyond her own tragedy and devoted herself to supporting the survivors of genocide.

The Rwandan genocide broke out in April 1994. The target was the ethnic group known as Tutsis and the perpetrators were the Hutus. The tensions between Tutsis and Hutus were not new; they had been raging ever since European colonisers had created divisions between the two groups. But this time the Hutu 'interahamwe' militia and army set about bringing a final solution to the 'Tutsi problem' by raping, battering and butchering. Despite being warned about the pending atrocities, the international community looked on and the genocide only ended when the Tutsi-led Rwandan Patriotic Front (RPF) managed to gain control of the capital, Kigali. Over the course of 100 days, an estimated one million men, women and children had been brutally murdered.[68]

Living in Kenya at the time, Mary Kayitesi Blewitt could only listen to the radio for information about what was happening to her homeland. When she finally managed to get into Rwanda on a Chinook Helicopter carrying NGO workers, she describes what she found as "pain, pain, grief, pain". Mary's immediate family had been forced to leave Rwanda in 1959 during an earlier period of Tutsi persecution but most of her family members had stayed. When Mary first arrived in Rwanda it was very difficult to find anyone she knew so she tended to the dead and listened to the survivors. As a way of managing her own loss, she threw herself into volunteer work to register those who had died and those who had survived. "There was no point in thinking about my own people because one million is bigger than fifty", she explained.

Whilst working as a volunteer Mary saw that there was a gaping hole in the management of the mass influx of aid organisations coming into the country. In response, she volunteered to manage and help establish an NGO Co-ordination Unit at the Ministry of Rehabilitation, despite the fact that, coming from an NGO background herself, she had developed a deep cynicism about relief work. She found most organisations arrogant, self-interested and uncontrollable. What's more, Mary was angered at their ignorance towards the issues surrounding survivors. To give you a sense of the types of survivors, reports estimate that during the genocide one third of children saw their families

CLOCKWISE:

SURF and AVEGA - a very strong partnership

AVEGA East – a regional meeting of widows

AVEGA East sell local handicrafts to raise funds

The medical centre on site at AVEGA East

murdered. The genocide left 34% of homes headed by women or orphans[69] and tens of thousands of women infected by HIV, victims of 'rape brigades' who deliberately spread the disease during the genocide attacks.[70]

Every day Mary would come face-to-face with the challenges facing survivors. Far from feeling fortunate for having lived, most felt survival was its own kind of torture. Widows and orphans were struggling to provide shelter and education for their dependants. Women who'd been raped were living with HIV and AIDs. Trauma left many suicidal. Yet despite these wounds, Mary began to see survivor-led organisations forming. One group in particular stood out – a small set of widows who regularly gathered to provide one another with peer support. Recognising their potential, Mary took them under her wing. She encouraged them to organise, form a constitution and register as a charity. Today the Association of Genocide Widows (AVEGA) has well over 25,000 members across the country.

After two years of hands-on work to support the genocide survivors, through AVEGA in particular, Mary returned to the UK where her husband and family were based. Compelled by an unrelenting sense of anger, she put her outspoken nature to good use by raising awareness about Rwanda at any opportunity. At one NGO conference in Dublin she was invited to the platform to say her piece but, when her fifteen minutes was up, she refused to leave the stage. Startled by her own indignation, she knew from that point onwards that she had to do more. Increasingly resentful of the way that international aid was being managed in Rwanda she decided: "I will set up a charity and I will show them that I can do it better. I am going to reach every single person who needs to be reached. And that's exactly what I did."

Working from her own front room with a donated computer, Mary set up *Survivors Fund (SURF)* in 1997. Its mission: to rebuild a sense of self and trust in humanity among the survivors of the Rwandan genocide. Since SURF started, Mary has supported 14 out of the 16 grass roots organisations working in Rwanda to support survivors. With SURF's support – both financial and non-financial – these organisations have responded to all the core needs of the estimated 300,000 vulnerable survivors of genocide. [71] From counselling to combat trauma to HIV treatment for rape victims; from new housing for those lacking shelter to scholastic support for orphans; from business loans for those seeking employment to... well, the list could go on and on.

SURF has also delivered a number of initiatives directly, the most memorable being 40 burial sites that provide a respectful place of rest for over 500,000 genocide victims. We were shocked to learn that, even now, bodies are still being discovered. Owing to the nature of the attacks, many of the dead were thrown into pits or buried where the militia saw fit. Slowly, as more and more perpetrators have come to justice, these locations have been revealed and SURF has made it its goal to ensure that surviving relatives have the chance to bury their loved ones with dignity.

But, as *one* woman working from the UK, how has Mary achieved all this? When quizzing her on her recipe for success, she listed the following three attributes: commitment, hard work and never taking 'no' for an answer. Mary brands herself as "a fighter" and her feisty ways certainly lend truth to that trait. Through sheer determination she has managed to bend the ears of many influential people, including Clare Short, Cherie Blair and David Cameron, and her efforts rarely fail to pay off. In 2004 she was invited to Downing Street for an evening with Cherie. Out of that was born a celebrity-studded campaign (bagging among others, Beverly Knight and Helen Baxendale) that led to DFID donating over £4 million for anti-retroviral drugs for rape victims infected with HIV.

SURF's operating model is also a key contributor to their success. Probably best described as a catalytic investor, SURF identify and invest in grass roots leaders who need funds and support to start up and grow their own ideas. Their core strategy is focused around capacity-building and their golden goal is to help every organisation become self-sufficient. And when it comes to dishing out the cash, they take an approach that most other foundations could learn a lot from. They're not rigid – they respond to any request from any survivor organisation; they're not precious – they broker relationships between those they work with and new funders; they're not remote – they have exceptionally close relationships with everyone they support.

SURF and AVEGA have worked so closely together that the two organisations' work is almost inseparable. Under SURF's strategic guidance they have decentralised their operations and vastly expanded the services they offer to widows. The centre piece of AVEGA is their eastern division which has developed under the leadership of Odette Kayirere, with Mary as a mentor and supporter. AVEGA East has built an incredible support centre that is staffed by 40 widows and orphans. To pay for the support services available, Odette has set up a number of profit-making business initiatives at the centre: a conference centre, guesthouse and restaurant. When we visited their site we were incredibly impressed by what we saw. Rwanda's largest bank was paying to use their facilities for a meeting, the regional group of widows were gathered in the courtyard for business training and the health centre was bustling with patients waiting to be seen.

Another pearl in SURF's portfolio of partners is Solace Ministries. John Gakwandi, the founder of Solace Ministries, survived the genocide by hiding with his family in a cupboard for 80 days. Afterwards he felt a calling to provide comfort and support to fellow survivors. Starting out as a small organisation, Mary guided their expansion and today they work in 59 communities. "Mary helped us to know more", John explained warmly. Among many things, SURF has provided Solace Ministries with the funds to provide new housing for hundreds of survivors. We took a trip out to visit one site where 60 homes were funded by SURF. Sandrine Mukayitesi welcomed us into her front room to share her story.

Sweet-natured and softly-spoken, Sandrine bears the physical scars of a brutal attack. At aged nine she witnessed the murder of her parents and was taken by the militia to the Congo as a human shield. Separated from her siblings, she explained that the men "mistreated" her. After a brave escape, she made her way to Kigali and lived in a derelict building with fellow orphans. Discovered by Solace Ministries, she was provided with vocational training and counselling, both of which helped to cure the persistent headaches she'd never been able to get rid of. Then in 2006 she was provided with a home, funded by SURF. "Since I got the house, I can struggle and survive better", she told us.

Sandrine Muayitesi

John Gakwandi, Solace Ministries

When you hear stories like these, you can understand why organisations like SURF have lobbied hard to try and raise financial compensation for survivors. But to date, this campaign has proven a lost cause. Keeping the genocide on the agenda of international governments and donors is a key challenge for SURF. As the years pass by, new priorities have arisen and the Rwandan government are keen to put the genocide in the past. They have even threatened to cut the small amount of funding they currently donate to survivor support. But Mary, who confesses herself that she has no interest in diplomacy, is very frank about the deep scars which are still tearing Rwanda apart. Mistrust and pain still run through the underbelly of society: "The survivors don't want to say it because the government will crack down on anybody who says there is not forgiveness and love between ourselves. We don't really have love."

It was saddening to hear Mary speak so openly about the ongoing struggles which face so many people but this did not belittle her achievements. Though Rwanda is far from healed, Mary has seen a change in the survivors she set out to help. "When I first met the survivors, they just wanted to die... I said to myself, I want to see them fighting. When they start fighting for themselves, for their rights, it will be time for me to go."

Confident that she could see a change in survivors' attitudes, Mary decided to step down from SURF in 2009. Though she was left exhausted by her emotional journey, she has since written a book and retrained as a complimentary therapist. If you're in need of some TLC and you've got a social conscience, we'd recommend you look up Mary Kayitesi Blewitt OBE. Her spirited personality is sure to mean your muscles will get a good pounding and more importantly, this is her latest social enterprise and profits from the session will be donated to survivors of genocide.

For more info visit:

SURF: **www.survivors-fund.org.uk**
AVEGA: **www.avega.org.rw/English.html**
Solace Ministries: **www.solacem.org**
Mary Blewitt: **www.marykblewitt.com**

Uganda

Capital City: Kampala
Population: 35,873,253
Area: 241,038 sq km
Official Languages: English
Gross Domestic Product (GDP): $45.9 billion
GDP Per capita: $1,300
IMF Poverty Index (of 190 countries): 174th

Key dates in history:

1830s Arab traders arrived in the 1830s. They were followed in the 1860s by British explorers searching for the source of the Nile.

1888 The United Kingdom placed the area under the charter of the British East Africa Company in 1888, and ruled it as a protectorate from 1894 until Uganda gained independence from United Kingdom on 9th October 1962.

1971 Idi Amin seized control of the country in a military coup in 1971. Amin's military rule lasted for the next eight years and killed an estimated 300,000 Ugandans. He forcibly removed the entrepreneurial South Asian minority from Uganda leaving the country's economy in ruins. Amin's reign was ended in 1979 when Tanzanian forces aided by Ugandan exiles counter attacked the country after a unprovoked Ugandan invasion.

1986 President Museveni has been in power since 1986. His presidency has included involvement in the civil war in the Democratic Republic of Congo and other conflicts in the Great Lakes region, as well as the civil war against the Lord's Resistance Army, which has been guilty of numerous crimes against humanity including child slavery and mass murder. Conflict in northern Uganda has killed thousands and displaced millions.

Alexander McLean

Giving prisoners a break

||||||||||||||||||||||||||||||||||||||||||||||||||||||||||||||||||||||||||||||||||||||||||||||||||||||||||||||||||||||||||||||||||||||||||||||||||||||||||||||||||||||||||||||||||||||||||||||||||

Alexander McLean, founder of African Prisons Project (APP)

" **On a gap year with a serious difference, Alexander McLean worked in a Ugandan Prison. Deeply disturbed yet hugely inspired, he went on to found an organisation which is redefining Africa's approach to imprisonment. *African Prisons Project (APP)* ventures to where so many will not go. Based in Uganda but also working in Kenya, they are bringing education, healthcare, justice and rehabilitation to thousands of prisoners who would otherwise be ignored.**

Alexander didn't set out on a gap year to work with prisoners and was originally working on a volunteer project with Hospice Africa Uganda.[72] He worked for three months bathing, clothing and supporting people coming to the end of their lives in Kampala's Mulago hospital and it was here that Alexander first met inmates from the local prisons. Frequently dying from starvation and dehydration, prison patients were usually grossly maltreated by hospital staff and left to die without an ounce of dignity. Appalled by the fact that these people were treated no better than animals, Alexander made it his mission to see what prison life was like. After weeks of persistence (understandably the prison services were somewhat dubious of this unusual 18 year old), he was granted permission to visit death row at Kampala's maximum security prison.[73]

We'd hazard a guess that Alexander is the first gap year student to take a trip to death row and the very fact he did sums up what an incredible guy he is. Unsurprisingly, what he found wasn't pretty. Living conditions were dire (over 300 people occupied a building built for 50), judicial rulings were questionable (inmates were condemned to death for crimes like kidnap, cowardice and treason) and the general wellbeing of prisoners was totally sidelined. Staff ruled by fear and the concept of rehabilitation didn't exist. But despite all of this, Alexander found he was greeted with immense warmth by the inmates, many of whom were similar to him in age. Having opened the door on something that most people freely ignore, Alexander felt it was impossible to just walk away.

By this time Alexander had already well extended his trip to Uganda (he was only ever meant to stay for two weeks) and his parents were growing increasingly uncomfortable with his African adventures. "My parents did everything possible to try and stop me from going. They thought I was throwing my life away for nothing", he told us. But, in his mind, his gap year was not complete. After a short trip back home to collect funds from the congregation at his local church, Alexander returned to the prison. With the help of inmates and staff, he refurbished the totally dilapidated health clinic. At this stage Alex-

105

CLOCKWISE:

High security gate outside Luzira Prison

Alexander with inmates living on death row in Luzira Prison

Alexander speaks to a prisoner on death row whilst a prison guard watches on

Our host for the day and former inmate Frank with the head of the prison staff

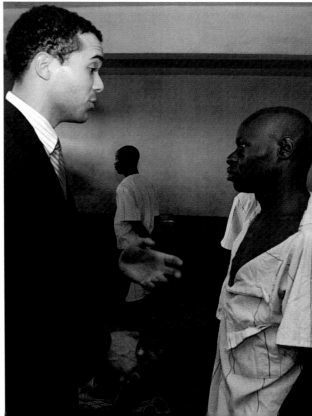

ander wasn't thinking about the long term impact of his work and was blown away by the transformation this simple project made. Over the next year, there was a significant drop in the number of deaths at the prison.

This one project set the ball rolling for many more initiatives aimed at improving prison infrastructure. Whilst in his first year of studying law at the University of Nottingham, Alexander managed to raise the funds to go back to Uganda and build its first ever prison library. We first met Alexander while running our own volunteer project at Nottingham. Not the kind of student you meet every day, we were hugely impressed by him and donating a few books seemed like the least we could do to help.

The more work Alexander did, the more he saw what was possible. His reputation was growing and other countries became open to his work. During his second year at university he convinced his father to join him in Sierra Leone where they refurbished the cells at a children's prison and then a few months later he took friends out to Kenya's Kamiti Maximum Security Prison where they did up the sick bay and kitted out a library. Fast becoming a prison expert, he also ventured on a research trip to Malawi, Zambia and Zimbabwe where he found the same pervasive needs. "I saw that people in prison were keen to learn, they wanted an education and health services. But more than anything they wanted justice", Alexander explained.

If you met Alexander your first guess might be that he's a lawyer – he wears smart clothes and he's the personification of articulate. But since graduating, law has been his part-time hobby and prison regeneration his full-time occupation. By now working as a registered organisation known as Africans Prisons Project (APP), Alexander returned to Uganda in 2007 and soon realised that the provision of infrastructure, namely libraries and health clinics, was only the first step in delivering lasting change within prisons. To build on this APP developed a holistic repertoire of services for inmates. They now cover education (adult literacy classes and book clubs), healthcare (sports clubs and counselling), justice (workshops to support inmates through the court process) and re-integration (advice and guidance on services available once released).

"I'm not very good at planning", Alexander admitted. As a result, APP's strategy has emerged as Alexander has learnt more and more about what works and what doesn't. One area which has sprung up as needing more attention is the integration of prison staff into APP's activities. Interestingly, one of APP's greatest challenges has been the attitude of prison staff who are naturally wary of APP's approach and envious of the facilities being provided to prisoners. To combat this APP have deployed a range of effective strategies, including a great new resource centre which runs out of their Kampala head office. Specifically for prison staff, as well as ex-inmates, the centre offers a fully-stocked library, computer skills training and a weekend club for wives.

It was here at the resource centre that we met our prison guide, Frank. Having lived on death row for many years, he was the perfect guy to give us a real insight into prison life and the impact of APP's work. A million miles away from being intimidating, Frank was softly spoken with a slight build and mottled grey hair. He had been sentenced to death for a fictional crime, designed to hide the fact that his 'wrong doing' was related to politics. For the first decade of his sentence there was no way for prisoners to appeal, but when Uganda abolished the mandatory death sentence in 2009,[74] Frank set about clearing his name through the Court of Appeal. After 23 years on death row, he was released.

Since being let out Frank has returned to the condemned section of Luzira Prison every week as an APP staff member and it was a true privilege to join him on a visit. Welcomed by prison staff and inmates alike, stepping onto death row was not one bit like we imagined. Yes, conditions were shocking but what was more overwhelming was the family atmosphere. A source of great wisdom, Frank explained that this community spirit comes from living among people who are all forced to accept their fate. Everyone we chatted to was brimming with warmth towards APP and spoke of Alexander as a brother. "Alexander is our friend, part of us in fact. He has done a lot for us", shared the inmate who oversees the APP library. In a bustling courtyard filled with people playing board games, we found a score sheet pinned to the wall with the title 'Sir McLean Draughts Tournament'.

The eagerness to learn displayed by most inmates was really striking, and thanks to APP, many have been able to really apply themselves, earning O-Levels, A-levels and even university qualifications whilst still inside. Alexander lists APP's educational feats among his proudest achievements and justly so. Thanks to a partnership between APP and the University of London, in 2011 55 inmates and prison staff applied to study for diplomas by correspondence from Uganda. Whilst on our tour of death row we met one of APP's first university students, Patrick. Thrilled to be accepted onto an undergraduate course in law in 2010, Patrick is planning on using his new expertise to help prove his innocence in his forthcoming appeal case.

APP currently supports one third of the 35,000 inmates in Uganda and has already expanded its reach to Kenya, Nigeria and Sierra Leone. The organisation has built a strong reputation for itself and as a result their services are in demand. Southern Sudan, Tanzania, Malawi, Zambia and Zimbabwe have all invited APP to work in their prisons. Alexander is keen to take APP Africa-wide and is working on a standardised package of model services which would allow APP to offer the best of their facilities at a reasonable cost to more countries across the continent (and maybe even beyond). Despite these grand plans for expansion, Alexander's ultimate vision is that APP will no longer need to work in these countries: "If we can establish model services... prisons will gain confidence in this new approach and then take it on for themselves."

Realising this dream will require a long term commitment from APP. Most African countries have been running their prisons according to brutal rules and regulations for decades, if not centuries. Having now visited over 70 prisons across the world, Alexander also knows that changing the lives of people in prison isn't straightforward. "There's no simple answer, no quick fix", he explained. That said, APP already seems to be shifting the mindset of the prison services. In recent years in Uganda, the government has started to provide support to selected prison schools and welfare officers are being introduced. Though nobody chose to credit APP with having influenced this, we felt sure there was a link.

APP is an exciting organisation. Most others doing hands-on work in prisons are small scale and have a religious foundation, whereas APP does not. What they've achieved already is groundbreaking and, should APP grow according

A resource centre provided by African Prison Project to prison staff and their families

Prison staff using a computer in the APP resource centre

to plan, they are on track to create a systemic shift in Africa's approach to imprisonment. Alexander will be pushing this shift every step of the way. Since he started APP, he's only ever received a small stipend and yet he's not one bit deterred. In fact, he's 100% dedicated to spending the rest of his life in this line of work.

For more information visit:

African Prisons Project: **www.africanprisons.org**

Laren Poole

A new war on terror

Laren Poole, co-founder of Invisible Children

❝ What do you get when you cross a rebel attack in northern Uganda with three innocent young Americans carrying a cheap video camera bought off eBay? Three *dead* innocent young Americans no longer carrying a cheap video camera bought off eBay? Nope. This is not a story which follows normal rhyme and reason. What this sequence of events actually gave birth to was a hugely successful charity that has taken America by storm: *Invisible Children*.

Jason Russell, Bobby Bailey and Laren Poole headed out to Africa in 2003 with the dream of making a documentary to show to friends and family back home in San Diego. Between them they had limited miles on their travel-o-meters and absolutely no experience in making films. But they had tons of testosterone, a thirst for adventure and a sack full of naivety – all the ingredients needed for the journey of a lifetime.

Dead set on throwing themselves in at the deep end, they went searching for danger. "We picked the most random place we could find that had a civil war", Laren told us. With the benefit of hindsight he now admits that their strategy was a little on the crazy side. "Looking back on it, it was really stupid. We could have definitely been killed."

Sudan was their chosen destination until their heads were inadvertently pointed in a new direction. Whilst travelling through Uganda, a truck in front of them was ambushed by the rebel group known as the Lord's Resistance Army (LRA). The three narrowly escaped death, those in the truck just yards in front of them did not. Unknowingly, they had walked into a war zone.

In 2003 the war between the LRA and the government of Uganda had already been raging for 17 years and it wasn't until 2006 that the LRA left northern Uganda, moving the conflict to neighbouring countries instead. Unlike most wars that are often rooted in tribal difference or land dispute, this conflict was deeply warped. The LRA leader, Joseph Kony, believed that he was possessed by spirits directing him to overthrow the government and enforce a rule of law based on the Ten Commandments. Unsurprisingly, he struggled to gain followers through conventional means and recruited an army by abducting children using brutal force.

Year after year families living in northern Uganda went to sleep at night fearing that the LRA rebels would storm their village, stealing their children for soldiers and their women for sex slaves. To avoid this terror thousands of children started a nightly commute into local towns where they could find

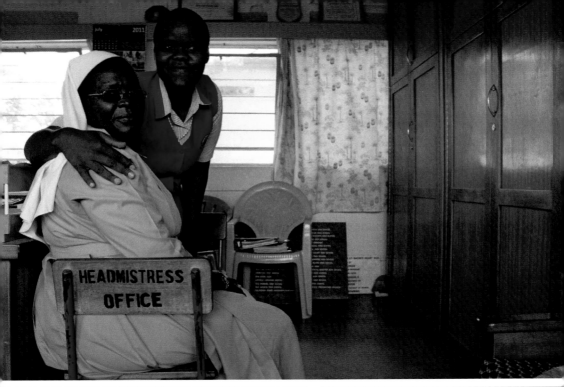

CLOCKWISE:

Sacred Heart Secondary School –
Sister Susan and Head Girl Mercy

Head Teacher of Gulu Senior
Secondary School, Florence,
shows off her building plans for a
new library and multipurpose hall
provided by Invisible Children

Development is well underway at
the Gulu Senior Secondary School

Mercy and Fred - both on
scholarships from Invisible
Children

TENDER DOCUMENTS-VOLUME I-I (DRAWINGS)
PROPOSED MULTI-PURPOSE BUILDING-LIBRARY AND HALL, Gulu. S.S

shelter and relative safety. After the ambush Jason, Bobby and Laren were forced to rest a night in the town of Gulu where they came face-to-face with this phenomenon. "The first time we saw it, it was bizarre. An exodus of young children. It was like a Hitchcock movie or something! It was crazy to see", Laren explained.

Appalled that a crisis of this scale was going unnoticed, the boys de-prioritised Sudan and made Gulu their base. Up for anything that would make their money last a little longer, they "lived in an abandoned building, peed in water bottles and stayed up all night to film the night commuters". But after two months they ran out of cash and were forced to bid farewell to their crowd of friends.

Struggling to turn their backs on Gulu, the boys agreed to find the funds to pay for the school fees of two brothers who had become their close allies. On the face of it, Jacob and Thomas were just local Gulu boys who loved to play football with their American mates. In fact, after being forced to watch the murder of their own brother, the two had run away from the LRA and were living in fear. As three young college kids from affluent families, Bobby, Jason and Laren knew they could find some school fees. Little did the trio know that they were in line to achieve a lot more.

Back at home and after a year pulling together a documentary, the boys set up some screenings for their local community which, to their astonishment, attracted a crowd of 3000 people and a decent chunk of donations. Having watched the film called 'Invisible Children: Rough Cut', it's obvious why it so quickly won over hearts and minds. A feat of creative genius, it's a perfect mix of laugh and cry footage. In between moving scenes of children crammed into their refuge centres, you meet the real Jason, Bobby and Laren whose antics (including killing snakes and slaughtering chickens) are left uncut. Not one bit try-hard, it's 100% authentic.

Until then, the boys thought that telling the story would leave them satisfied that they'd done their bit. But their viewers all left the screening with one remaining question: What are you going to do about it? "Everyone else out there was meant to do something about it!" Laren recalled with laughter. No such luck. A dawning realisation hit the three boys and they grabbed the moment. They decided to stop being three young kids who stumbled into something. Instead they transformed into changemakers, devoted to stopping the LRA.

In 2005, Invisible Children (IC) was founded as a non-profit organisation and since inception their strategy has remained simple. They tell stories to change lives. Groups of young volunteers (a.k.a. 'roadies') tour the United States and screen creative and compelling documentaries about the LRA and the devastation they leave behind them. Their plea is always the same: Give us your Talent, your Time and your Money. Through donations and merchandise sales, to date Invisible has raised nearly $50m. "That's a freaking lot of money", Laren said before we did, still amazed by their fundraising prowess.

Unlike many broad-reaching NGOs, their funds are hyper focused on one mission. IC wants to stop the LRA, see the leaders brought to justice and help their victims to get a fresh start. Thanks to the strength of their public support (an estimated ten million people have now seen IC's movies), they have become an influential mouthpiece. They worked closely on peace talks held with the LRA in 2008 and although the talks were unsuccessful, they've kept the pressure high on the American government. Thanks to the advocacy efforts of hundreds of thousands of young people and the leadership of a few key members of congress, in 2010 President Obama signed a bill into law that required the US to design a strategy to apprehend Joseph Kony.

The IC founders have even managed to bend the ear of President Obama directly in a face-to-face meeting at the White House. They decided to spend their precious ten minutes with Obama retelling Jacob and Thomas' story. In response, Obama sent back a typically presidential message. "Tell those boys that the President of the United States knows about this and he's going to do something", he said. Since then, the US have sent troops to Uganda to advise forces within the region on how best to manage the ongoing struggle against the LRA.

The LRA has now retreated from northern Uganda, so IC focuses its work there on supporting victims and investing in the next generation. Educational support is central to their services and, as of December 2011, includes the provision of scholarships and mentoring to over 840 secondary and university students, infrastructural and capacity building support to 11 carefully selected secondary schools, and a Teacher Exchange Programme between Uganda and the US. Their work within rural communities is equally impressive and includes the establishment of Village Savings and Loans Associations (VSLA) groups, which support families returning from displacements camps, an adult literacy programme and a tailoring project known as Mend which supports females formerly abducted by the LRA.

When we visited IC's work in Gulu, we were struck firstly by how polished it was and secondly by how thoughtful it was. IC has always advocated the approach of 'Ugandans helping Ugandans' and their team is sensitive to the every need of their community. Sister Susan, Head Mistress at Sacred Heart Secondary School for Girls, was the first to point this out: "What I found impressive is the rounded support they give. They look at the entire needs of the students." Over 130 girls were abducted from the Sacred Heart Secondary School during the peak of insurgencies and many of their students are nursing the wounds of war; so too are the women working at the Mend centre. But with 24/7 support from a local social worker based in their office and a steady income from the beautiful bags they produce, they are beginning to rebuild their lives.

However, as many begin to put their lives back together in northern Uganda, just over the borders in Democratic Republic of Congo, Central African Republic (CAR) and South Sudan, the LRA continues to tear lives apart. Conflict is an ongoing challenge and Africa continues to rank as the world's region least at peace.[75] More than one fifth of the continent's population remains directly affected by conflicts.[76] But wherever Kony goes, IC will follow. They have expanded their operations to Congo and CAR and introduced a raft of new initiatives to support those being affected. Dedicated to LRA disarmament, they are also treading potentially dangerous ground by encouraging rebels to defect. By using innovative radio messaging they're showcasing the stories of ex-soldiers who've escaped and been given amnesty, in the hope it will encourage others to do the same. Remarkably, it's working and from the bottom up, IC is chipping away at the might of Mr Kony.

Milka makes chic new bags at the Mend social enterprise in Gulu

Laren hands-on and hard at work in Democratic Republic of Congo

"We're not leaving until Joseph Kony goes away", Laren told us emphatically. Perhaps somewhat harshly, he added that until this happens, IC is technically a failure: "We've had some great wins along the way, but we're a failure overall – we haven't yet accomplished our big goal." When your cause is so focused on one long term goal, it can be hard to justify your progress on a monthly or annual basis. However, we felt IC's niche focus is exactly what makes it so compelling. Those who give their time, talent and money in support of IC's work are totally clear about where their donations are going and to what end, however distant it might appear at times. All too often you just don't get this kind of transparency.

We left Gulu with a resounding respect for Invisible Children and its founders. Though IC has attracted a lot of attention (they have even featured on The Oprah Winfrey Show), Jason, Bobby and Laren's efforts are ego-less. Despite all the recognition for their work there was no hint of arrogance. The clearest demonstration of this is their decision not to cling on to CEO status; all three have handed over the responsibility of global operations to others they deem more qualified.

"I'm not CEO because the CEO has to do things that I'm not trained to do", Laren told us. Though Laren no longer plays a role in the day-to-day operations of the charity, both Laren and Jason still spend their time making movies. In actual fact, these roles are by far the most fundamental because it's their fresh, eclectic style which has made IC such a success. Check out their films and you'll see exactly what we mean and, even better, you'll get a free copy to pass on to a friend. Never an opportunity missed, we swear that IC has thought of it all!

For more info visit:

Invisible Children: **www.invisiblechildren.com**

Kenya

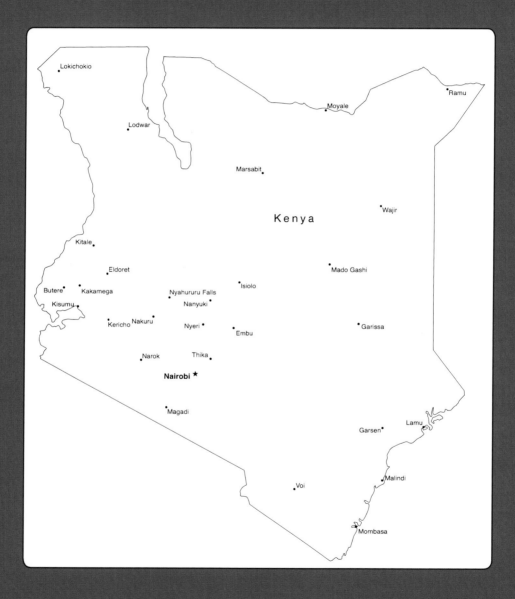

Lokichokio

Ramu

Moyale

Lodwar

Marsabit

Kenya

Wajir

Kitale

Eldoret

Mado Gashi

Isiolo

Butere
Kakamega
Nyahururu Falls

Kisumu
Nanyuki

Kericho Nakuru
Nyeri
Garissa

Embu

Narok
Thika

Nairobi ★

Magadi

Lamu

Garsen

Voi

Malindi

Mombasa

Capital City: Nairobi
Population: 43,013,341
Area: 580,367 sq km
Official Languages: Swahili, English
Gross Domestic Product (GDP): $71.5 billion
GDP Per capita: $1,700
IMF Poverty Index (of 190 countries): 153rd

Key dates in history:

100AD Arab traders first arrived around the 1st Century AD and by the 8th Century Arab and Persian settlements sprouted along the coast.

1885 A German protectorate was established in 1885, followed by the arrival of the Imperial British East Africa Company in 1888. Germany handed its coastal holdings to Britain in 1890.

1952 A rebellion against British rule led to a state of emergency from October 1952 to December 1959.

1963 Nationalist President Kenyatta formed a government shortly before Kenya became independent from the United Kingdom on 12th December 1963, on the same day forming the first Constitution of Kenya. The Republic of Kenya was later declared on 12th December 1964.

Recent Despite being a relatively stable and peaceful country since independence Kenya is regularly rocked by scandal and political corruption.

David Kuria

Toilet business

||||||||||||||||||||||||||||||||||||||||||||||||||||||||||||||||||||||||||||||||||||||||||||||||||||||||||||||||||||||||||||||||||||||||||||||||||||||||||||||||||||||||||||||||

David Kuria, founder of Ikotoilet

" In general going to the toilet whilst you're travelling in Africa is not an experience you look forward to. To be totally frank, it's so bad that invariably it makes you gag. But in Kenya, ask anyone for the nearest *'Ikotoilet'* and all your dreams come true. For just five shillings (3p) you get to do your business in a spick and span public loo. What's more, once you're done you can top up your phone, buy a cold coke or get your shoes shined. The vision of David Kuria, this simple social business aims to challenge toilet taboos and make sanitation sexy. Sound a bit crazy? Not one bit. Poor sanitation kills millions every year and David's 'toilet talk' strategy is saving lives.

"In most parts of Africa, you can't talk about sex and you can't talk about toilets. It's considered very private", David explained to us. Let's be honest, conversations about personal hygiene are uncomfortable the world over. But when every 20 seconds a child dies of poor sanitation[77], it's not an issue which can be ignored. Most international NGOs do register the importance of this problem and along our journey we saw an abundance of toilets installed by World Vision[78] and the like.

"I don't think NGOs will ever support any real service delivery impact", David said. Having worked in the NGO space for numerous years, David had every right to hold to this personal point of view. Before his Ikotoilet venture, he set up and ran a new government department aimed at co-ordinating the NGOs working in Kenya's slums. After that he ran the Nairobi office of an NGO that does hands-on development work in urban settings. But, after eight years of drilling boreholes and building toilets, he saw the challenges facing Kenya's slums growing worse, not better. Convinced there must be another way of doing things, he quit his comfortable NGO job and decided to go it alone.

With no real plan and a limited amount of savings, David set up a registered business called *Ecotact* in 2006. When trying to justify the sanity of his actions to his wife, all he could say was that he wanted to tackle a pertinent issue in an innovative way. Whilst his family worried for their future security, David beavered away at a borrowed desk, and after six months he had hatched a master plan. "Sanitation is more important than independence", Gandhi is famed to have said. After a thorough review of the challenges facing his people, David decided Gandhi was undoubtedly right.

So improving sanitation became his chosen mission, but what about the innovative approach? Totally disenchanted by tokenistic toilet-building, Da-

CLOCKWISE:

David with the world's great and the good

The pledge card by IkoToilet which led to their Guinness World Record

Queues forming outside one of many IkoToilets in central Nairobi

A kiosk attached to an IkoToilet to generate revenue

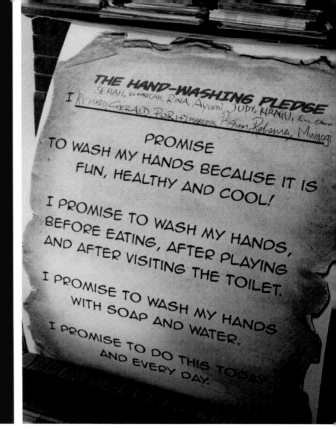

vid set his sights high. "I wanted to re-invent the whole sphere", he told us. After months of hard graft and research, the Ikotoilet concept was born and with it three core objectives:

1) To transform the architecture of the toilet

An architect by training, David believes all buildings should be beautiful. "No one has given any thought to the toilet as a piece of art", he said to us not even breaking into a smile. Determined to prove that with beauty comes respect, David purposefully designed every block of toilets (each block known as an 'Ikotoilet') to be a striking landmark. Using funky shapes and bright colours, it's fair to say the Ikotoilet isn't easily missed. What's more, both the staff and the customers take time to keep the loos in great condition, proving David's mantra that if you build something beautiful, people will want to take care of it.

2) To implement a business model that disrupts the status quo

For just 3p, an affordable price for all, the general public can go to an Ikotoilet and access clean, safe and hygienic sanitation facilities. A service that before Ikotoilet, simply didn't exist. This might not sound revolutionary but here's the twist. The Ikotoilet block is also known as a 'Toilet Mall'. The space surrounding the loo block is rented to local businesses that provide a range of services like hair cutting, shoe shining and money transfer. Drawn in by the opportunity to advertise to a captive audience, bigger businesses also pay for wall space to promote their brands.

Income from entry fees, rent revenue and advertising deals covers all the overheads of each Ikotoilet and leaves enough left over to repay David's investment loan. In fact, within five years each Toilet Mall will be turning a tidy profit. Aside from being a nice little money-making scheme, the beauty of this model is that it removes the stigma around stinky toilets, creating instead a space where communities can convene. In turn, this places important pressure on the Ikotoilet staff to keep their standards high and their facilities 100% stench free!

3) To get people talking about sanitation and hygiene

Using innovative mass media campaigns, David tackles cultural taboos which keep toilet business a 'hush hush' topic of conversation. To date he has recruited Miss Kenya to serve toilet tissue to customers, at the same time talking to them about the link between hygiene and beauty. He has also brought in other public figures to do the same, including the Vice President, key religious leaders and Kenya's top comedian. In 2010, he took an even wackier approach. He brought together 18,302 children, 1050 adults, 40,000 litres of water and 23,000 bars of soap at one venue to break the Guinness World Record title for 'Most Number of People to Wash their Hands in One Day'. Unsurprisingly, this campaign and others successfully keep hygiene in the headlines. "We have got people talking about toilets", David told us positively, explaining that driving behavioural change is the objective which underpins everything within the Ikotoilet strategy.

The success of Ikotoilet in Kenya has come as a shock to David, especially

as Ikotoilet almost failed to get off the ground. In 2007, when David was trying to get started, he was turned away from every Kenyan bank for a loan.
"They would give me an audience but when I told them it was about a toilet,
they would look at me as if there was something wrong." On the brink of
chucking in the towel, David managed to convince Acumen Fund (an investment company solely focused on social ventures)[79] to take a chance on him,
granting him a $750,000 loan in three instalments. Luckily, this risk paid
off. Within just three years, 50 Ikotoilets have been installed in 20 munici-
palities across the country and in 2011, Ikotoilets expect to receive ten million customers, an average of 30,000 per day.

Importantly, Ikotoilet is also providing employment to 150 staff and, much
to David's delight, people are clamouring to get a job in the company. "This
is not a toilet team, it's an Ikotoilet Team", David told us, explaining how
his staff are employed in "sanitation hospitality". Determined to create
a dignified place of work, each of the operators at an Ikotoilet receives a
uniform and a tailored training programme. Ingeniously tackling sanitation
taboos from every angle, these basic provisions support the shift in mindset that David is trying to create. The job of a toilet attendant has actually
become desirable. Now I bet there are not many countries which can make
that claim.

But Ikotoilet can make many claims. Not only have they completed an almost clean sweep of social enterprise awards, including recognition from
World Economic Forum, Ashoka, Clinton Initiative, World Toilet Organisation and Global Water Challenge,[80] but they are also Kenya's single largest
toilet roll consumer! This might not build their environmental credentials,
but Ikotoilets make every effort to keep themselves green. They use water-
less urinals, low flush toilets and water-saving taps. They even try to make
use of human waste by converting it into bio gas for cheap cooking fuel and
fertilizer for community gardens.

If these awards tell you one thing, it's that Ikotoilet has a bright future. David
estimates that Ikotoilet is only responding to 10% of the demand in Kenya,
providing ample space for growth over forthcoming years. Within Kenya,
he's also branching out into sanitation for schools. Using donations to cover
the initial building costs, he's already built ten Ikotoilets on school grounds
and will use corporate advertising to pay for the ongoing overheads. Hoping
to shape the views of the next generation, each new installation is also supported by an education programme which promotes hygiene, sanitation and
good health. Not content to stop at the Kenyan borders, David is also looking at scaling Ikotoilet across the whole continent. With the financial support of East African Breweries, a ten toilet trial is about to launch in Uganda,
and there are plans in the pipeline for Tanzania, Ghana and Liberia. This
expansion is essential as currently it's estimated by the United Nations that
only 60% of people in Sub-Saharan Africa have access to basic sanitation.[81]

Having travelled through much of Africa, we can vouch for the fact that the
demand for these facilities is sky high. Now you could argue that governments should be encouraged to take responsibility for providing these basic
facilities themselves. But David's experience of working with bureaucrats is
sad proof that politicians are not willing to fill this gap. David approached
the Kenyan government for financial support to help him scale his business
much more quickly. He also proposed that all Ikotoilets be handed over to

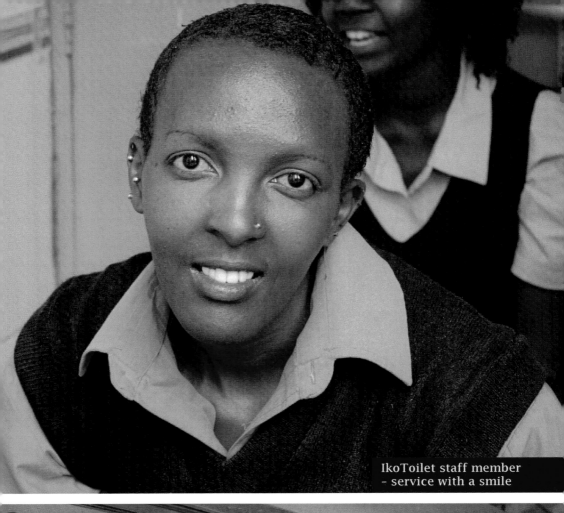

IkoToilet staff member
- service with a smile

IkoToilet customers
get their shoe shined

local councils after a period of time. Unfortunately, all of his proposals have fallen on deaf ears and the government is willing to do nothing more than publically endorse his work.

Apathetic politicians are a massive frustration for David and countless other social entrepreneurs. But in all honesty, Ikotoilet's response to the improvement of sanitation is far bigger and far better than any government could likely provide. Though David can't yet measure it, he knows that his facilities and campaigns are having an impact on the incidence of sanitation-related disease. When we visited an Ikotoilet in central Nairobi for ourselves, the long queue of customers was evidence enough that people are taking onboard his messages. In Swahili 'Ikotoilet' literally means 'There is a toilet'. After our Ikotoilet visit, we decided we wanted to add a few extra words. There is a toilet... which is changing the world.

For more info visit:

Ecotact: **www.ecotact.org**

Nick Moon

Africa can feed the world

Nick Moon, co-founder of KickStart

" Many believe that the current TV images of starving and malnourished people in Africa's Eastern Horn are a vision of the years ahead. But imagine a future where Africa, instead of being a case study in suffering, had become a saviour in the frenzied battle for food security. Nick Moon, co-founder of *KickStart*, adamantly believes that African agriculture is an untapped resource in the fight to feed the world. "All that land, all that water and all that labour... there's not a problem here, there's a solution."

When you travel through Africa, the vast expanses of open space make the cities feel like mere pin pricks on the landscape. Staring out of bus windows we noticed the huge amount of fertile land, some of it in cultivation but much more of it not. When we met Nick Moon, he was quick to explain that "Africa's true competitive advantage is agriculture". The trouble is that right now, not only is a lot of land left untouched, but the agricultural practices of small holder farmers means that land is not being used effectively.

Plant your crops and wait for God to bring the rains. This is the test of faith lived out by most subsistence farmers. As admirable as this fatalistic belief in God might be, it doesn't make for good business. When the rains come (if they come at all) everyone takes their harvest to market where supply outstrips demand and profits are therefore very low. What's more, once the rainy season passes food becomes very scarce again, forcing farming families into a vicious cycle of feast and famine.

Co-founded in Kenya in 1991 by Nick Moon and Martin Fisher, KickStart is dedicated to breaking this cycle. KickStart develops agricultural technology specifically geared towards the needs of small holder farmers so they can work themselves out of poverty quickly, efficiently and sustainably. Though they have a range of products on sale, by far the most successful is their Money-Maker Water Pumps which allow farmers to irrigate their land all year round.

To date, KickStart has sold over 180,000 pumps across their operations in Kenya, Tanzania, Mali, Burkina Faso and through partners in Malawi, Zambia and Mozambique. For every 100 pumps sold, they estimate that 91 of them are used to transform the productivity of a farm by at least 400%. As a result hundreds of thousands of farmers are now growing crops for both internal and external markets, creating enough food to feed their families and earn an income which lifts them above the poverty line.

Nick and Martin have developed an array of agricultural products over the last 20 years but water pumps, they insist, are the most important of them all.

CLOCKWISE:

Johnson and his family demonstrate the Money Maker Pump in action

Nikki gives it a go

Nick shows us some of KickStart's earlier inventions

Nick proudly gives us his pitch

"There may be other issues like seeds, soil fertility, access to markets, post harvest storage... but the primary bottleneck is water management. If you can capture, store and lift water onto your crops... you can grow more food, more intensely, more often." As we travelled out to visit a MoneyMaker Pump in action, Nick explained to us how he and Martin came to become such experts on agricultural development.

A rampant socialist in his teens, at 17 Nick jacked in his formal education to train as a skilled woodworker. A high-flying student at the time, this move to join the modern-day proletariat showed real commitment to the Socialist cause (and upset his parents a lot). After re-training in woodwork he set up a social co-operative which evolved into a specialist company for the restoration of Georgian homes. However, Nick felt his business was too much of a divergence from his values. "It troubled me that we were becoming joiners for the gentry", he explained. So in 1982 he sold up, moved to Kenya with Voluntary Services Overseas (VSO)[82] and has never gone back to live in the UK.

Posted to a small village in Western Kenya, Nick's VSO experience was a steep learning curve. "I learnt a lot about what the world looks like through the lens of a small holder farmer", he said, explaining how tough life was for the rural community he had lived in. After three years, he moved on to work for a well-known international NGO where he met Martin Fisher, a Stanford super brain who originally came to Kenya to pursue his academic interest in the link between technology and poverty. From what Nick told us, Martin's academic credentials definitely put Nick's unfinished secondary school career to shame!

Together Nick and Martin worked on just about every kind of development intervention, from building rural water systems and schools to creating job training programs. Yet, although Nick and Martin had a great time in the NGO world, they felt scarred by the pattern that emerged. Nine times out of ten, when they handed over a project to be run locally it would collapse. When this happens, it's easy to point the finger at a lack of commitment from local people, but Nick would argue that it's usually short-sighted NGOs that appear to be the cause of this recurring problem. They are accused of growing so obsessed with their own priorities that they lose sight of the genuine needs of the people they're trying to help. "It's a lot of money, a lot of work and a lot of expertise for very little social return", Nick told us, convinced that conventional NGOs have had their time.

Determined to develop a new model for fighting global poverty, Nick and Martin started to look at the alternatives. What they concluded was simple but it required a softening of Nick's socialist ideals. They realised that, just as is the case anywhere, the number one need of poor families in Africa is to find a way to make more money and that social interventions must reflect that. From this insight, *ApproTEC* (later renamed KickStart) was born.

Their model was, and still is, to develop, launch and promote simple money-making tools that poor entrepreneurs could use to create their own profitable businesses. Nick and Martin started by designing a press for making stabilised soil building blocks. However, despite the product proving popular, it didn't hit the mark for their vision. "It meant people could build stronger houses for less money but we kept on asking ourselves, how do we really generate wealth?" Nick said. They challenged themselves to go further.

After years of searching for how they could truly help people at the 'bottom of pyramid', they decided to focus solely on small-scale farmers and in 1997 the first MoneyMaker was developed. Since then the pump's design has undergone numerous iterations but it always follows the 'plug and play' principle. A local farmer can pick up a MoneyMaker Pump in their local store for a very competitive price ($35 or $95 depending on the model) and start their new irrigation regime that very same day. Even better, if they can't afford the investment outright, KickStart offer a microloan service to reduce the burden.

We went to see a MoneyMaker Pump in action at a local farm on the outskirts of Nairobi. Johnson, a fit, youthful looking farmer, was working with his family on a plot of French beans for sale overseas. His MoneyMaker Pump was in full swing and Nick explained to us how the process works. The farmer digs a hole up to eight metres deep until they hit the water table lying just beneath the surface. The pump, which is operated manually like a step machine in the gym, sits next to the hole with two long hoses coming out of it. When you start pumping, water is sucked up one hose and pumped out the other. Though Nikki's efforts to work the pump were feeble (months of no exercise had taken their toll!), this design is infinitely quicker and more efficient than the bucket and rope alternative which many farmers still use.

"I have become a serious businessman and this is my office", Johnson told us whilst he looked out across his rugged plot. Before he invested in a Money-Maker Pump he rented 0.2 acres of land and watered his crops using a bucket and well. After being lent a MoneyMaker Pump by a neighbour, he was able to significantly increase his yield and make the transition into growing high value commercial crops. He now owns two MoneyMaker Pumps, rents 2.7 acres of land, has bought 0.9 acres of his own and grows everything from bananas to water melons and maize. Chuffed to be setting an example to his community, Johnson makes enough money to send his three children to school and is about to buy a motorbike.

KickStart is not the first or only organisation to produce these kinds of pumps (also known as 'Treadle Pumps'). Thanks to the collective efforts of many organisations such as IDE, SK Industries and Practical Action[83] significant improvements are being made in small-scale irrigation.[84] Africa as a whole continues to be the world's most food-insecure region[85] but the United Nations believe that increased roll-out of low-cost treadle pumps could significantly boost food security across the African continent.[86] In order for this to happen, it's essential that the organisations driving this change are scalable and sustainable. And that's where KickStart's market-based solution really stands out.

Whilst KickStart helps people like Johnson to set up their own self-sustaining businesses, KickStart itself is not a profit-making company. In 2011 they spent $10m, one third of which is was covered by income from product sales and the remainder by funders like the Bill & Melinda Gates Foundation.[87] Importantly, however, KickStart never intends to become a profit-making entity. Instead they want to stimulate a market for water management products and encourage new competitors to enter the game. "Others might come in and do it better than us and we don't care, we want them to do it", Nick explained. At this point, KickStart plan to shift their focus onto new products and markets.

As yet, they haven't attracted any real competitors into the market as most organisations in this field are producing lower volumes of pumps and invari-

One of hundreds of hardware stores selling the Money Maker Pumps

The next generation of Money Maker Pumps are under creation

ably give them away free. Consumer demand is growing but reaching a critical mass takes time, especially when your products require people to adopt a whole new mindset. KickStart's marketing strategy has to convince people who've relied on the rains for centuries that a pump is better. What's more, if KickStart want the market for water management products to be sustainable, they have to showcase the fact that farming can be lucrative and stem the flow of young people leaving their villages in hopes of a more comfortable city life.

These challenges are exactly why KickStart's sales strategy is very hands-on. In Kenya, for example, KickStart has a team of 65 regional sales representatives who work with people face-to-face. Key to their approach is local demonstration events held on farms where people come together and see the MoneyMaker Pump in action. Using traditional sales methodology, the sales reps use these events as an opportunity to convert their hot prospects and build their list of future clients. Every effort is made to promote the brand with caps and T-shirts – always a popular give away and we too weren't allowed to leave the office without a MoneyMaker baseball cap.

This business savvy approach is reflected in every part of KickStart's operating model. But, as with their iterative approach to product design, it's taken time for the KickStart business to reach today's level of sophistication. Nick's decision to complete an MBA was a key turning point for the organisation, enabling them to lay much stronger business foundations. All the same, KickStart has been winning awards left right and centre for years, including recognition from Skoll and Schwab, as well as Bill Clinton. In 2003 they also picked up another nice little accolade – TIME Magazine's European Hero Award and in 2012 they were recognised in Forbes Magazine as one of the Top 30 Social Enterprises in the World.

Hero status is big. But we think it's justified. KickStart estimate they have helped 600,000 people out of poverty (and that's a conservative number). Even better, they see this as just the start. Nick told us that within the next 15 years he believes, "Every single person of a responsible age in Africa will know what agriculture water management technology solutions are out there, and what value they can offer them, and be able to walk down to their local store and invest."

Nick is not a man of few words and every question we asked him opened up a long debate over the best way to tackle social change. Luckily, he's a hugely fascinating guy so we never got bored...in fact he's currently planning to move on from KickStart and we definitely think he should become a lecturer. He left us totally convinced that where a cause or need can be linked to a market-based solution, it should be. What's more, he left us dreaming about a future where Band Aid's 1980s hit 'Feed the World' becomes a massive irony. With help from KickStart, it might just turn out to be Africa that ends up feeding us all.

For more info visit:

Kickstart: **www.kickstart.org**

Erik Hersman

Disaster or demonstration, what you need is a map

Erik Hersman, co-founder of Ushahidi

66 From earthquakes to uprisings, you name it; the last twelve months
have been witness to them all. And when a disaster strikes, what one
thing does everyone look for? Information. If you're in the thick of it,
you need to know what to do, where to run and how to hide. If you
find yourself in such a crisis without the information you need, here's
a top tip. Go online and download *Ushahidi.* Launched by four talented
techies, the simple piece of kit allows you to organise yourself and others,
ensuring that everyone can access accurate and up-to-date information
during their time of need.

In December 2007 the Kenyan presidential election results were announced.
The incumbent President Mwai Kibaki was given victory over his opponent, Rai-
la Odinga. Claims about rigging of the results caused voters to go on a violent
rampage and a political, economic and humanitarian crisis erupted. Former UN
Secretary, Kofi Annan, arrived in the country nearly a month after the election
and successfully brought the two sides to the negotiating table. But reports
suggest that the impact was lasting; the BBC revealing that 1500 people died
and 250,000 were displaced.[88]

When this post-election violence kicked off, Erik Hersman, Juliana Rotich, David Kobia and Ory Okolloh came together online and started a conversation.
Acquaintances from the blogging world, these four virtual friends could have
easily felt powerless. They were dispersed around the globe and had never met
face-to-face as a group before. But these were not ordinary circumstances, nor
ordinary people. The group were united by two important things which meant
they couldn't turn their backs on the crisis: firstly, they were all Kenyans who
loved their country; and secondly, they were all technology fanatics who believed that software could save the world.

Erik Hersman kindly gave us his time whilst we were in Nairobi. Born in America but raised in Kenya, he describes himself as an "import" but calls Kenya his
home. We were intrigued to meet Erik as his accolades reach far and wide. He
writes two hugely popular blogs, the White African and Afri-Gadget, which together receive up to 50,000 unique visits a month (to put this into perspective,
amazon.co.uk receives 24,000,000 unique visits per month).[89] He regularly
shares the stage with the founders of Twitter™, Facebook™ and Google™ and
he's a Senior Fellow at TED™ (a non-profit organisation offering events, conferences and the TEDTalks video website).[90] By all accounts he has the credentials
of a Silicon Valley don. But the events of 2008 took his career off on a tangent.

CLOCKWISE:

Erik Hersman

The M-Lab – incubating the next generation of tech entrepreneurs

A screenshot of the Ushahidi Platform – go online to try it yourself

Erik hosting one of many speaking events in his office Hub

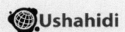

PRODUCTS

You are Here: Home / Products

Tools for democratizing information, increasing transparency and lowering the barriers for individuals to share their stories.

The Ushahidi Platform

The SwiftRiver Platform

Crowdmap

We built the Ushahidi platform as a tool to easily crowdsource information using multiple channels, including SMS, email, Twitter and the web.

SwiftRiver is an open source platform that aims to democratize access to tools for filtering & making sense of real-time information.

When you need to get the Ushahidi platform up in 2 minutes to crowdsource information, Crowdmap will do it for you. It's our hosted version of the Ushahidi platform.

All content ©2008-2012 Ushahidi
Contact Us
Privacy Policy
Website Feedback

About Us
Our Mission
The Team
Testimonials
FAQ

Get Involved
Volunteer Registration
Language Translations
Donate

Help & Support
Help Forum
Resources
Development Wiki
Bug Tracker

 Blog Facebook Twitter Vimeo Flickr

"We'd always claimed that technology allows us to overcome inefficiencies", Erik told us. "If we couldn't have proven that during the most inefficient time in our own country's history then we would have had nothing to stand on." And this is why Erik and his fellow pioneers used their collective technical know-how to lend a hand back home. Following the suggestion of one team member, they decided to collate and map the news alerts coming from various sources, building a clearer picture of the unfolding events online. In a quick fire decision based partly on the availability of .com addresses, they called their new software 'Ushahidi', a Swahili word which means 'testimony'. This word also happens to be impossible to pronounce... so here's the idiot version: "oo-shah-hee-dee".

Thanks to their pre-existing fan base (as bloggers they were already very well known), they managed to attract attention to Ushahidi very fast. As soon as they posted a message to promote their site, they started to attract 75,000 to 100,000 unique visitors a day. Over the weeks that followed the group developed numerous iterations of the Ushahidi platform, adapting it so that local people could submit their own reports via the web or using their mobile phones. Volunteers would then work to approve and verify the information, building a much richer story of the incidents going on throughout the country.

To walk you through what this would have looked like for a user, if you'd seen a riot in your neighbourhood, you would text the details to the Ushahidi telephone number. After a short delay, your report would be plotted on an interactive map on the Ushahidi website, along with other reports submitted across Kenya. To stay up to date with the situation you would sign up to receive news alerts to your mobile phone, or go online to view the latest version of the map.

With 45,000 active users contributing to the Kenyan website in this way, Ushahidi proved to be a success. It also planted the seeds for much more, acting as a catalyst for the founders to carry on working together. When they started to receive requests for replication in other African countries, they realised that their new innovation could be of great use to millions around the world. Unintentionally they had struck upon a new way to channel information during a crisis – from the bottom up.

"The technology was nothing new. We just created another mash up. The innovation was in the humanitarian element. We were shaking the foundations of the way information flows", Erik explained. Instead of having to rely on information which comes top down from the authorities or media sources, the beauty of Ushahidi is that it harnesses the powerful knowledge of the people on the ground. It encourages society at large to come together, share what they know and build a picture of events which has greater breadth, depth and objectivity.

By August 2008, the team of four founders quit their jobs and morphed Ushahidi into an organisation with a broader remit. Their aim was to become specialists in developing free and open source software for information collection, visualisation and interactive mapping. This description might sound intimidating to a luddite but here are two important words of note: 'Free' – Ushahidi develops software that is free for all to download and requires no registration, username or password protection so that the barriers to entry are kept as low as possible, and 'Open source' – Ushahidi develops software that is open for all to add their input, meaning that it's constantly being improved by its community of users.

Over the last three years, the original Ushahidi programme has been developed to better suit people's varied levels of technical expertise. For those born without the technology gene, a hosted version of the program known as *Crowdmap* is now available (this means that everything you need is available to you online without having to download any software onto your computer). Much faster to get started, this solution has proven very popular, with around 1000 people using it per month. Another piece of software called *SwiftRiver* has also been developed which, in layman's terms, helps to make sense of vast amounts of incoming information. This one, however, is strictly for use by people *with* the gene. Nikki lost track of Erik's explanation of SwiftRiver after an estimated five seconds!

To date there have been 17,000 deployments of the Ushahidi solution and, interestingly, it's used by people in a huge variety of ways. The team have analysed trends in its use and discovered that it works best in 'hot flash scenarios' i.e. events which take place over a short period where people have a strong demand for co-ordinated information such as natural disasters, elections, political uprisings and terrorist attacks. In fact Ushahidi has played a co-ordination role in most of the major global crises of recent months and years, including the Haiti Earthquake, the Japanese Tsunami and the Arab Spring Uprisings.

"What this really is, is an extension of what the Red Cross should be doing but online", Erik explained, an analogy which made a lot more sense once we'd been given some working examples. To share a couple with you: in Libya the UN used Ushahidi to collect and co-ordinate information from 400 volunteers across the country. This provided them with an accurate view of the violence and attacks, allowing them to target their response efforts more effectively. After the Haiti Earthquake, Ushahidi was used both by the emergency response agencies, and the people on the ground. In this case its purpose evolved over time. Used initially to identify missing people, it was later used to track the number of people who had died and then the outbreak of disease.

As Ushahidi is open to all, this does mean that the perpetrators of immoral acts could use it to co-ordinate their efforts, too. Terrorists, for example, could use Ushahidi to map out their target sites and consolidate information from their informants. The Ushahidi team are aware that the multi-purpose nature of their programs could lead people to use it for dubious purposes but they follow the same line as all major software developers. "It's hard to be objective but the technology *is* fairly neutral", Erik explained. "I could use Gmail or Word to organise terrorist activities as well." Thankfully, Ushahidi has only ever been used once for "iffy purposes" as Erik called them, which was during the recent revolution in Egypt.

In general, people use Ushahidi to co-ordinate information for themselves. But in some cases, when the situation on the ground is highly complex, as, for example, after the Haiti earthquake, Ushahidi use their paid team and their huge cohort of volunteers, to source, approve and verify all the incoming information and then build it into a map. You could argue that this brands them a disaster relief NGO with a difference but Erik disagrees. "If someone calls us an NGO, we correct them right away. We're a non-profit tech company much more like Mozilla." (Mozilla are the company who own Firefox, the internet web browser program.)

Like it or not, in terms of the funding model, Ushahidi does run much like an NGO, as 80% of their costs are covered by private foundations. However, the

Dozens of micro social enterprises hot desk in the office Hub

Erik's colleagues make the most of Ushahidi's free wifi

remaining 20% of their funds are raised through contract work for external clients, making Ushahidi look much more like a company. Nike, for example, have approached Ushahidi about building them an interactive map which would help them to track grievances raised by sweat shop workers (a potentially marvellous plan; let's hope they pursue it). Also, the team are looking at significantly reducing their dependency on foundation funding by introducing a broader suite of chargeable services.

The culture of the company is also totally business-focused. "We work fast and loose", Erik explained, the kind of words more frequently heard from those with a business background. Ever since Ushahidi was first used in Kenya, the company has stuck to the principle that everyone involved has to be a self-starter capable of responding to any situation on their own and at speed. "If there's a problem you solve it, you don't go to someone else to help you", Erik said plainly. This is essential when you can't just knock on the door of your boss. The Ushahidi team works entirely virtually, holding only one face-to-face meeting a year.

Ushahidi only has 15 paid staff but they are supported by a huge community of volunteers who tinker with their software and are on-call when something big kicks off. Still, they're nowhere near the size of the Googles of this world, and they plan to keep it that way. "We're small so we can be disruptive!" Erik said, pointing out that larger organisations stay well away from anything this controversial. Whilst 'disruptive' might sound rather militant, in techie-speak 'disruptive technology' is used to describe innovations which shatter the status quo. In that way, Ushahidi is a perfect example of a 'disruptive' design. "We just really love creating software that disrupts the world in a way which helps ordinary people", Erik said with glee.

The Ushahidi team plan to continue the exponential growth of their non-profit tech company and they are also supporting others to do the same. Compelled by the desire to give something back to their volunteer community and uncover the next Ushahidi, they have set up two initiatives to hot-house technical innovation. The I-Hub, an incredible community space right in the centre of Nairobi, provides a range of resources for its 4500 members including free access to the internet, training, pre-incubation advice and the best cappuccinos in Kenya! The M-Lab is for I-Hub graduates who have a serious business idea which needs further incubation and investment. With seven ideas currently under development, the M-Lab is sure to produce another prize-winning company.

Meanwhile, the Ushahidi solution couldn't be timelier. As we were writing this article, riots were raging across the UK, bringing home to us the fact that no country is immune to unrest. However, knowing that Ushahidi is on hand to help make sense of crises to come, makes us feel a lot more reassured. When considering how to tackle social and environmental challenges, we think more people should experiment with technological solutions. The world needs more people like Erik and his partners, so if you're an emerging talent in technology, why not give Erik's story some serious thought and join this techie crusade.

For more info visit:

Ushahidi: **www.ushahidi.com**
White African Blog: **www.whiteafrican.com**
Afrigadget: **www.afrigadget.com**

South Sudan

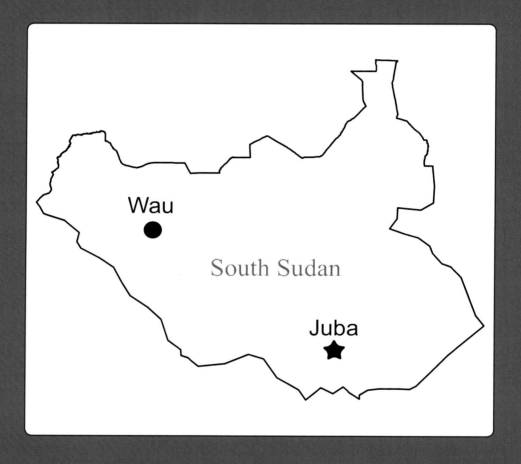

Capital City: Juba
Population: 10,625,176
Area: 644,329 sq km
Official Languages: English
Gross Domestic Product (GDP): N/A
GDP Per capita: N/A
IMF Poverty Index (of 190 countries): unknown

Key dates in history:

Middle Ages	Both ancient Egypt and Arabs in the middle ages raided Sudan for its natural resources.
C19th	In the nineteenth century the native Azande people fought the French and the Belgians to maintain their independence.
1870s	Egypt attempted to control the region in the 1870s, establishing the province of Equatoria, but Equatoria ceased to exist as an Egyptian outpost in 1889.
1924	For much of the early 20th Century Sudan was effectively administered as a British colony with Egyptian support. From 1924 the British rulers had a policy of running Sudan as two essentially separate territories, the more educated, developed Muslim north and the underdeveloped uneducated black Christian south. In 1947 the British tried and failed to join South Sudan with Uganda.
1956	Sudan gained independence from Britain and Egypt in 1956.
2011	A referendum was held in January 2011 to determine if South Sudan should declare its independence from Sudan, with 99% of the population voting for independence from 9th July 2011.
Now	South Sudan is at war with at least seven armed groups in nine of its ten states, with tens of thousands displaced. Joseph Kony's Lord's Resistance Army (LRA) also operates in a wide area that includes South Sudan.

Emmanuel Jal, photo ©Dave Watts

War child turned international rap super star

Emmanuel Jal, founder of Gua Africa

" How does a surviving child soldier from South Sudan come to count Alicia Keys amongst his friends? No, this isn't another story of a celebrity ambassador adopting a child in need. This is the story of Emmanuel Jal, an extraordinary international rap star who, unlike his counterparts, uses music for a moral purpose. Against all the odds, Emmanuel survived a traumatic childhood and now uses his talent to put right the wrongs in his own past and to change the future for other young people. As he sums up in the first line of his hit record *War Child*: "I believe I've survived for a reason, to tell my story to touch lives."

Sudan's past is punctuated with periods of unrest, but the second civil war, which ran for over 20 years and officially ended in 2005, was devastating. Roughly two million people died as a result of war, famine and disease caused by the conflict, making it one of the highest civilian death tolls of any war since World War II.[91] To make it worse, both sides (the central government and the rebel forces) enlisted tens of thousands of children into their ranks;[92] Emmanuel Jal included.

Emmanuel was seven when his mother was killed by soldiers loyal to the government. His family took desperate measures to try and protect Emmanuel from any more traumatic consequences of war. They sent him to join the thousands of children travelling to Ethiopia where it was believed to be safer. But the risks were high and on the way, Emmanuel and many others were intercepted, snatched by the Sudan People's Liberation Army (SPLA) and taken to military training camps in the bush.

After several years of harrowing combat on the frontline, Emmanuel escaped along with 300 others known as 'The Lost Boys'. Few survived their torturous three month trek to safety but Emmanuel's bravery was rewarded when, at age 11, he was rescued by a remarkable British aid worker called Emma McCune. Emma smuggled Emmanuel to freedom in Kenya and enrolled him in school, but it wasn't long before Emmanuel was forced to fend for himself once again. Tragically, just months after meeting Emmanuel, Emma died in a fatal car crash.

By now I'm sure you're beginning to see quite why Emmanuel's story is so extraordinary. Emmanuel admits that, after Emma passed away, rebuilding his life whilst living in the slums was an uphill struggle. But thankfully he found something which bolstered his resilience – music. "When I was in Kenya I was stressed out and confused; I didn't know what to do so I used to go to church and see

CLOCKWISE:

One of the brand new classrooms in Gua Africa's Emma Academy in South Sudan, photo © Gua Africa

Team of students we met in Nairobi on a Gua Africa scholarship

Emmanuel Jal, photo ©Geoff Pugh

Gua Africa, photo ©Gua Africa

people sing and dance. The music was good. So, even though I didn't like the pastors, I started going to church every Sunday because I liked the music."

Despite having no musical background, from this point on Emmanuel sought inspiration and direction in music and became a huge hip hop follower. Religion also became central to his life, making P-Diddy's hit, *Jesus my best friend*, a firm favourite tune. "Even gangsters can sing songs to God!" he told us with animation. Aged 20, Emmanuel took centre stage for the first time and shared his first song, *All we need is Jesus*, with his congregation. "We were rocking the church and it was explosive", Emmanuel said in a voice tinged with surprise. The song became a huge hit in Kenya and received airplay in the UK.

As well being a full-time occupation, music became a form of therapy for Emmanuel. Sharing his personal philosophy about the power of music he told us, "It's the only thing which can speak to your heart, your mind and your soul system. It can influence you without your permission." Compelled to use his music to help others as well as himself, he started to write lyrics which lobbied for political change and called for peace and independence in South Sudan.

In 2004, he released his first album, *Gua*, meaning both 'good' in Nuer (a South Sudanese tribal language) and 'power' in Sudanese Arabic. Rapping in Arabic, English, Swahili, Dinka and Nuer (I wonder how many languages Eminem can rap in?), the album was a storming success. The title track, also called Gua, was a number one hit in Kenya and gained huge traction with everyone affected by the conflict in Sudan. Here's a sample of the lyrics:

In my homeland, Sudan
Not one sister will be forced into marriage
And not one cow will be taken by force
And not one person will starve from hunger again
I can't compare to anything
The time when people will understand each other
And there's peace in my homeland, Sudan
                         Gua, Emmanuel Jal

If you type 'Emmanuel Jal Gua' into YouTube you can watch and listen to a version of this song, which is ten million times better than reading the lyrics on a page. Emmanuel's style is totally unique. Poetic, soulful and rich with African beats, it falls under the banner of hip hop but couldn't be further from listening to Jay Z. This alternative style, combined with a social agenda which comes out of the depth of his experiences, is precisely what excites people about Emmanuel. After being invited to perform in the UK at Live 8 in 2005, a music producer seized on Jal and since then his music has featured on an album alongside that of Coldplay, Gorillaz and Radiohead, and his singles have been used both on TV (namely *ER*...very exciting) and the big screen (namely *Blood Diamond*...even more exciting). In 2008 Emmanuel performed at the 90th birthday concert for Nelson Mandela and in early 2012 his third album will go on mass release.

All of Emmanuel's songs promote the message of peace over persecution, a theme which resonates far and wide and has led hundreds of thousands of people to listen to his work. But more than just influencing the world through album sales, Emmanuel has used his music in a myriad of ways. Most significantly, a lot of the money he has made through music has been re-invested in building a better Sudan. "I never used to enjoy spending my money on myself", Emmanuel told us modestly. "I like to use it to put somebody in school."

Even before Emmanuel was earning a decent wage, he used money from odd jobs like washing cars to help street children and fellow refugees to pay their school fees. To formalise his efforts he founded the organisation *Consolidated Association for South Sudanese (CASS)*, that later became a registered charity called *Gua Africa*. "I am so passionate about education because aid has crippled us and if we want to save my people, education is the only way", Emmanuel said persuasively.

Based in South Sudan and Kenya, the core programme at Gua Africa is the provision of shelter, sponsorship and support for young people rescued from refugee camps. We met Matthew, one of the 32 young people currently being supported, at one of Gua Africa's homes in Nairobi. Having lost his siblings to war, at age 11 his parents forced him and his only remaining brother to flee Sudan. After more than a year of travel by foot and transit truck, they settled at Kakuma Refugee camp in Kenya and joined a school run by the United Nations (UN).

Gua Africa has strong working links with Kakuma and it was from here that they rescued both Matthew and his brother, bringing them to Nairobi for a better education. Both worked hard, determined to make the most of their new opportunity despite joining classes with people half their age, a certain challenge to any young person's pride. Matthew is now studying Surgery and Human Health at university and throughout his journey, Emmanuel Jal has been his role model: "We appreciate him for what he's doing. We normally listen to his music as it's a lesson to us. It gives us a lot of encouragement."

Matthew and his peers all aim to return to South Sudan once they have completed their education, a life choice which Gua Africa actively supports. By the time this happens, Gua Africa will have finished their first community education centre in Matthew's hometown of Leer. Named the Emma Academy in memory of Emmanuel's saviour, this school is a response to the hugely pressing need for education in South Sudan, where UNESCO estimates that less than 2% of children are completing primary school and where secondary education is available at just 40 schools [93] (Note: South Sudan has a population of 9 million and is 2.5 times bigger than the UK, which has nearly 4000 secondary schools).[94]

Despite his busy workload and being based in the UK, Emmanuel's personal commitment to Gua Africa is striking. In order to raise funds for the Emma Academy he completed a 661-day 'Lose to Win' fast. Eating only one meal a day, he donated the money he saved to the project and encouraged others to do the same, raising over $200,000. "I thought I was that famous that I would raise money quickly", Emmanuel said to us, admitting he underestimated how long it would take him to reach his target.

Undeterred by the two years he spent living on limited calories, Emmanuel had us in stitches over his next fundraising master plan which he's called the Modern Day Nomad Campaign. "I will leave my house and close it and until I raise $1.5 million I won't go back in!" he said in between bursts of laughter. Having gained an insight into Emmanuel's eccentric ways during our interview with him, we felt assured that no matter how long it takes living as a nomad, Emmanuel would reach his goal.

Emmanuel Jal leading his 'We Want Peace' campaign

we want PEACE

The Time to Prevent Another Genocide is Now!

The 'We Want Peace' campaign moto, photo © Kemi Davies

Although $1.5m might sound like a lot of money, it matches the size of Emmanuel's vision for the future. In the years to come he wants Gua Africa to "be able to help anywhere that is in need", and he plans to do that by "setting up different scenarios to inspire the world". Beyond his music and his charitable works, Emmanuel has already experimented with almost every medium there is to get his message across. As well as being an artist, he's an actor (a documentary about his life called *War Chid* was made in 2008), an author (his autobiography was released in 2009 and he's written feature articles for newspapers including the Guardian) and he's an activist.

As well as supporting existing campaigns and causes like Amnesty International and Oxfam, Emmanuel has his own personal activist's agenda. Most recently he launched his own *We Want Peace (WWP)* campaign to coincide with the referendum in South Sudan. This global campaign has a bold aim: to raise awareness of the fundamental principles of justice, equality, unification and conflict-prevention, through the power of music, worldwide.

Once again demonstrating the powerful potential role of music in social change, WWP is centred around a new release featuring Alicia Keys, George Clooney, Richard Branson and Kofi Anan. The call to action underpinning WWP is about asking people to take a few simple steps to promote peace and once signed up to the campaign you're christened a 'Peace Soldier' (nice touch). The campaign aims to have one million Peace Soldiers by the end of 2012. When we read through the jaw-dropping list of celebrity supporters behind WWP, we pondered how Emmanuel remains so modest about his work. When asking him what he was most proud of he offered a sheepish response, unwilling to big himself up. "I don't really know, I'm just doing what I do. I just want to make a difference that's all."

But *On the Up* is about celebrating the incredible success of social entrepreneurs like Emmanuel Jal, so let us do some boasting on his behalf. Now it's probably a step too far to credit him with ensuring the referendum process in Sudan remained peaceful, but it certainly would be fair to say that, together with his army of 'Peace Soldiers', his messages had a significant part to play. In January 2011, over 98% of the population of South Sudan voted in favour of independence and in July, South Sudan became an independent state.[95] Like so many South Sudanese, Emmanuel sees this landmark divide as an exciting opportunity for the years ahead.

Whilst the future of the country lies in the shaky hands of a new government, it's people like Emmanuel Jal who are really making a difference. Emmanuel's work just shows what real dedication from a public figure can achieve – he is keeping South Sudan present in the hearts and minds of millions of his followers and helping to ensure that the young people of this newest of nations have the skills and opportunities they need to stop history from re-writing itself.

For more info visit:

Gua Africa: **www.gua-africa.org**
Emmanuel Jal: **www.emmanueljal.org**
We Want Peace: **www.we-want-peace.com**

Egypt

Capital City: Cairo
Population: 83,688,164
Area: 1,001,450 sq km
Official Languages: Arabic
Gross Domestic Product (GDP): $515.4 billion
GDP Per capita: $6,500
IMF Poverty Index (of 190 countries): 122nd

Key dates in history:

3150BC The unified kingdom of Egypt was founded in 3150 BC by King Menes, leading to a series of dynasties that ruled Egypt for the next three millennia, building the many pyramids and wonders of Ancient Egypt. For 3,000 years Egypt was the world's superpower.

C1st Christianity was brought to Egypt by Saint Mark the Evangelist in the 1st century but later Egypt was absorbed into the Islamic Empire by the Muslim Arabs in 639 who ruled until the Ottoman empire invaded in 15th Century.

1798 A brief French invasion of Egypt led by Napoleon Bonaparte began in 1798. The French were kicked out in 1801 by Ottoman, Mamluk, and British forces. Out the chaos that ensued Ottoman power in Egypt was finished and Muhammad Ali, an ambitious and able leader, established a dynasty that was to rule Egypt until the revolution of 1952. In later years, the dynasty became a British puppet.

1922 Despite gaining independence from the United Kingdom on 28th February 1922, British rule effectively lasted from 1882 until 18th June 1953 when Egypt became a republic and British advisers were expelled.

1967 In 1967 Israel invaded and occupied Egypt's Sinai Peninsula and the Gaza Strip, which Egypt had occupied since the 1948 Arab–Israeli War.

1973 In 1973, Egypt, along with Syria, launched a successful surprise attack against the Israeli forces occupying the Sinai Peninsula and the Golan Heights to regain part of the Sinai territory Israel had captured 6 years earlier.

2011 On 25 January 2011, widespread protests began against the then president Mubarak's 30 years regime.

Raghda El Ebrashi

A student army gets Egypt to work

Raghda El Ebrashi, founder of AYB-SD

" **Egypt's first employment agency for the underprivileged.** *Alashanek Ya Balady for Sustainable Development (AYB-SD)* **now works with 1000 students across Egypt to provide training, coaching and employment opportunities to thousands of people a year. Starting out young hasn't made her journey easy but Raghda has weathered every storm and remains certain about her ultimate goal: to end poverty in Egypt and beyond that, the world.**

We arrived in Egypt within weeks of the revolution that toppled President Mubarak's 30 year military rule over the state. More developed than any other country we'd travelled through, the extent to which the tourist trappings can create a smoke screen to conceal a country's challenges is amazing. Unemployment, for example, is a major issue for young people. With 81 million inhabitants, Egypt is the Arab world's most heavily populated country and also one of its youngest: two thirds of the population are under 30.[96] This under 30s age group makes up 90% of the country's unemployed, totalling over 8 million young people out of work.[97]

Like so many developing nations, the contrast between rich and poor in Egypt is stark and the interaction between those at either end of this spectrum is almost non-existent. Born into a privileged family, Raghda El Ebrashi didn't experience anything outside her well-to-do lifestyle in Cairo until a school trip took her to Sharkeya, a region 100 kilometres from the capital with much lower standards of living. It was here that she met a total stranger who changed the course of her life.

Raghda was 12 when she met Om Fathy, an old mother who invited Raghda into her own home. To Raghda's horror she found just a tiny room with no roof, set in the middle of a field. "Where is the air conditioner?" she enquired out of innocence. Then Om Fathy introduced Raghda to her children, explaining that she rarely had all seven boys in the home at the same time as its limited space meant they had to sleep in shifts. Despite the lack of material possessions, Raghda was charmed by this unfamiliar world, shocked to find it in many ways richer than her own.

Clearly a feisty young teenager with well-formed views, she returned to Cairo with an ultimatum. Unless she was allowed to visit Om Fathy and her children every week, she would refuse to go to school. After one week of playing truant, her parents buckled and up to the age of 16, Raghda spent every waking

CLOCKWISE:

An AYB job creation campaign

Raghda hosts an AYB Seminar

Raghda signing a funding contract with Nissan

Inside the AYB office

hour waiting for the weekends when she would go back to Sharkeya. "It was there I learnt the meaning of fun", she beamed.

As well as having hours of fun, Raghda also realised she had a capacity to make a difference. Simple things like teaching Om Fathy's boys how to write using sticks in the sand made her realise that she could help underprivileged Egyptians to live a more sustainable and dignified life. So she set about developing her own interventions, including literacy classes and art lessons for people in poor communities. Just to clarify, Raghda was doing this between the ages of 12 and 16. Puzzled at how Raghda made this work, we challenged her: "Did people take you seriously?" we asked. "No of course not", she replied smiling.

When Raghda entered university at age 16 (the age at which most enter the university system in Egypt), her vision was clear but her challenges remained the same. "By the age of 16 I wanted to run something on my own. I wanted a national academy where young students could contribute to community development. I wanted to revive the youth to do something for Egypt. But it was not permitted for a 16-year-old to open an NGO and become the CEO."

The walls of the AYB-SD offices in Cairo are adorned with quirky quotes that sum up their ethos, such as, "successes come in cans, failure in can'ts". True to this motto, Raghda has never let bureaucracy deter her. As a fresher she went out to universities across Cairo, asking fellow students to volunteer their skills by running training courses for the underprivileged. Focusing on the capabilities needed to get people into employment, such as English and IT, students came on board in their droves. Soon she had 100 young people dedicated to playing their part in a workforce the like of which had never been seen before.

Students being students, they weren't quiet about their work and you might well ask "why should they be?" But when you live in a world surrounded by watchful eyes, it pays to be inconspicuous and sadly, in the minds of a controlling state, those who speak out must be silenced. "Let's just say we had a long term relationship with the State Security", Raghda said coyly. Right from the start, the government tried its hardest to close down AYB-SD, but Raghda refused to succumb to their intimidating tactics.

After a long period of being regularly detained by the state security, Raghda was thrown a lifeline by a sympathetic minister. He invited AYB-SD to manage a project distributing food and shelter to 10,000 people in a deeply deprived area of Cairo. If she pulled it off, the permission she needed to run AYB-SD would be granted. Innocent and unprepared, Raghda rallied her students to the challenge and, although they just about finished the job, she admits it was a massive shambles. Unsurprisingly, Raghda was left feeling totally defeated: "I have to tell you the truth. I decided to let it go. I decided I would volunteer for other NGOs because I couldn't see how we'd ever get the permissions."

Interestingly, most social entrepreneurs we've met have admitted that they'd almost chucked in the towel at some point. These aren't people who give up without a fight but when you look at the size of some of their challenges, it's easy to see how they could appear insurmountable. When people give themselves the freedom to fail they shouldn't be judged; it can take more courage to quit than to carry on.

Yet, despite Raghda's worst fears, the project was judged as being far from a failure, and the minister, satisfied with AYB-SD's aims, signed a stack of papers which granted them the status they needed to operate without interrogation. In this case Raghda had managed to triumph over a hugely bureaucratic state, a battle which many others in her situation have failed to win. Their new status allowed Raghda to take her vision nationwide and in 2002 she launched a campaign at ten universities across the country and began to formally franchise her model. With guidance from the Cairo HQ, affiliated student groups started to take root around Egypt, all focused on delivering training to support underprivileged people trying to get into work.

It's hard to understand how she found the time, but Raghda did manage to leave university with a bachelor's degree in Business Administration. By now somewhat skilled at multi-tasking she decided to run AYB-SD as a volunteer and work a full-time career on the side (amazingly, this is still what Raghda does today). Carving a career path was harder for Raghda than she had imagined and her first real job, selling soap for a multinational conglomerate, turned out not to be her bag. "I couldn't stand it. I lied for money", she laughed. But she finally found her feet in lecturing and also embarked on a PhD, becoming the first Egyptian ever to write a thesis on social entrepreneurship.

This further period of study led Raghda to start questioning AYB-SD. "We asked ourselves questions like 'will someone with better computer skills really be able to get a job and escape the cycle of poverty?' No. The answer to every big question like this was no. It was a shock." So Raghda went back to basics. Starting with the telecoms industry, she made enquires about the skills and capabilities they really needed. The Sales Manager of a multinational telecoms company working in Egypt made their requirements very clear: "Why on earth do I need him to know English? He's working in areas where people don't speak English. I need a salesperson to know sales."

Knowing that this telecoms company was keen to grow their rural presence, Raghda negotiated a deal. She would train up ten people from poor communities in sales and subsidise their wages if the company gave her new recruits a chance. Subsidising the wage was a matter of principle, as Ragdha deemed the company's £30 per month salary unacceptably low. Though apprehensive, the company agreed to give it a go and were thrilled when the AYB-SD's trainees outperformed everyone's expectations. Now a key partner for AYB-SD, in 2009 the company requested 400 more sales people and agreed to pay a salary of £75 per month plus commission. Result.

This model has now become the norm for AYB-SD. Using their network of student franchises (now totalling ten across the country), they review industry needs and train people from marginalised communities in the skills required. Training topics include administration, hospitality, textiles, housekeeping, nannying, sales and much more. They then match people to jobs, negotiate fair contracts and provide ongoing coaching support. In 2010/11 they placed 2,000 people in employment, partnering with an impressive list of private sector brands like Pepsi, Vodafone, Aramex, Shell, Nissan, Samsung and others.

To complement this, AYB-SD is also committed to nurturing entrepreneurship. For people interested in starting their own small businesses, they pro-

Catchy phrases line the walls

Above the Line Campaign

vide training in areas like pottery, textiles, mechanics, and mobile phone maintenance. They then offer loans, alongside ongoing capacity building advice, to help people start up and scale up their enterprises. This approach makes them considerably more holistic than many microfinance projects and to date they have given out 1000 loans to deserving individuals who might not otherwise have been offered this chance.

But for Raghda this is just the tip of the iceberg. With 44% of the Egyptian population earning under $2 per day[98], she believes AYB-SD must think big. In fact just days before we visited AYB-SD, they launched their Foq El Khat (meaning 'Above the Line') campaign with the goal of empowering ten million Egyptians to rise above the poverty line by the year 2020. This is brave and bold but so too is Raghda, and her list of backers demonstrates just how many people believe she can deliver. She is an Ashoka Fellow, has been hailed an 'Arab World Social Innovator' (by Synergos), a 'Young Global Leader' (by the Schwabb Foundation and World Economic Forum) and has been ranked in numerous polls as one of the most influential social entrepreneurs in Egypt and the wider world.

When it comes to funding her vision, Raghda's done well to spread her revenue over a portfolio of different income streams. She describes three core ways in which AYB-SD raises money: firstly, 'Mission Centric Money' – income from companies which pay for their employment services; secondly, 'Mission Related Money' – income generated through their own social businesses, including a private training firm which works in both the public and private sectors; and finally, 'Mission Unrelated Money' – money raised through business ventures that capitalise on their skills but have nothing to do with their cause, for example an in-house design company which does branding and graphic design for a range of clients.

Spreading her income in this way has helped Raghda not to get too bogged down in the stress of fundraising. Instead, she loses sleep over the big issues. "I have challenges all over the organisation every day but they are trivial if compared to our main target: the alleviation of poverty", she said. To us, this sums up Raghda's style. Constantly preoccupied by the needs of others, she recently refused a stipend offered through her Ashoka award, asking them instead to donate the money to someone else more in need of the support.

When Raghda told us this, we laughed out loud. She's the first social entrepreneur we've met mad enough to give away money. But Raghda is very principled about creating a 'people organisation' which relies on itself and not on her being at the helm. "If I die tomorrow and one of the staff resigns because I died, that means I failed", she told us. Whilst this is an admirable aspiration, we would suggest that both AYB-SD and Egypt need Raghda as much as ever. Having just overthrown dictatorial rule, Egypt is a country where visionaries like Raghda will be needed to shape a better future, where the people come first and political dictatorships are laid to rest.

For more info visit:

AYB-SD: **www.ayb-sd.org**

Sherif El Ghamrawy

Living on a lettuce leaf in a garbage bin

||||||||||||||||||||||||||||||||||||||||||||||||||||||||||||||||||||||||||||||||||||||||||||||||||||||||||||||||||||||||||||||||||||||||||||||||||||||||||||||||||||||||||||

Sherif El Ghamrawy, founder of Basata and Hemaya

" When you arrive at *Basata*, an eco-resort off the coast of the Gulf of Aqaba in Egypt, it's a bit like walking into the movie *The Beach* just without the rainforest. Slap bang in the middle of nowhere, this perfect piece of paradise ticks all the boxes – crystal clear sea, pristine white beaches and sweeping mountain scenes. Over the last 30 years Basata has been a birthplace for change, all driven by its founder, Sherif el Ghamrawy. A social soldier who wants to transform the region of Sinai, Sherif makes every social and environmental issue his business and every guest at Basata his new best friend.

Egypt's eastern region of Sinai is famous for lots of reasons: Sharm el Sheik, the mecca for all-inclusive holiday deals; Mount Sinai, the mountain where Moses received the Ten Commandments; and the fractious relationship with their previous occupiers, Israel. But it wasn't any of the above which attracted Sherif el Ghamrawy to move here in the 1980s. He came here looking for a place which would make him feel human again – something which the frenetic, smelly city of Cairo did not deliver.

Explaining his feelings, he told us with a warm smile, "I was living in a nice villa with a big garden and I had a good job in the city centre but I didn't see the point. My father asked me, 'Sherif, why?' I explained to him that living in Cairo is like living on a lettuce leaf in the middle of a garbage bin." A civil engineer by training, Sherif's family had high hopes for his professional future. But Sherif had his heart set on a different life. Basata is an eight hour drive from Cairo along a road with nothing but sand for scenery.

Now, a lot of people sit and dream about running away from city life and living on a blissful beach, but how many do you know who've done it? Well, Sherif is one of those brave few for whom courage outweighs caution – something we've seen in a lot of social entrepreneurs. In 1982 he set up shop on a small cove on the east coast of Sinai with a vague idea to build a place where cultures could collide and the environment comes first. In contrast to Cairo, he named it Basata, meaning 'simplicity'.

Though he didn't know it at the time, Sherif actually built one of the world's first eco-resorts which, at 30 years old, must surely be one of the longest running, too. What started out as a couple of bamboo huts and bucket showers is now an extensive range of accommodation, including glorious chalets just perfect for romantic retreats. Water runs through a recycling system and the

costly process of desalination (taking the salt out of the sea water) is only carried out when needs must. Candle light prevails once the sun has gone down and the sea breeze acts as nature's air con.

Basata is a self sufficient 'bubble' in the desert serving every need of Sherif's family, his guests and the wider community. Beyond the huts and chalets, there's a school, mosque, animal farm, veggie garden, handicrafts shop and bakery. But despite all this expansion, the ethos at Basata has always remained unchanged. All mod cons like TV and internet are forbidden and the sense of community is key to its success. People come together at meal times to cook and every evening there's an option to share in a feast of local foods – one of the best meals of our entire trip. For all of this, Basata has won much recognition both in Egypt and beyond. In 2006 Sherif won a prestigious Responsible Tourism Award and in 2009 he was nominated for the Condé Naste Environmental Award.

Unfortunately, however, the developers now neighbouring Sherif's land are not so commendable. For 99% of the hotel companies now operating along this coast, profit comes before people and concrete before community. "I don't like to use this comparison but it's like raping the land. Tourism is just fashion. When this fashion passes what are we going to do with all of this concrete?" Sherif said with genuine grief plastered across his face.

Moments later he called over a staff member and started shouting in Arabic whilst pointing at the sea. Entirely confused at first, we pieced together what was happening. Fishermen were spreading their nets over the coral reef which stretches along the coastline by Basata. His colleague ran to the shore and started shouting. The fishermen rushed away and Sherif sat down and sighed, "Always the fight, always the fight".

Sadly both the international hotel chains and many of the local people don't share Sherif's strong belief in respecting the environment, which is why, in 1996, he started an NGO called *Hemaya*, meaning 'protection'. Unlike many areas of Africa, this is not a location where many NGOs operate. Ever since Israel pulled out of Sinai in 1979 and handed it back to Egypt, the region has been left in limbo, with the government only showing an interest in tourism. This lack of state support means that organisations like Hemaya are left desperately to try and plug the gaps.

Hemaya's flagship project, which has been running since the organisation started, is their solid waste management business. Put simply, they collect rubbish, sort it and sell the recyclable stuff. They have contracts with hundreds of hotels spanning the coast and two sophisticated sorting centres manned by more than 30 staff. Here they keep what they can sell and give away things of use to others. Organic waste, for example, goes to local farmers for animal fodder. Whatever is left over is safely disposed of and, unlike many, they never burn their rubbish or tip it into the sea.

It was this project that brought Sherif's work at Hemaya into the limelight. He's won recognition from Ashoka, speaks at international conferences on solutions to waste management and has been asked by the Egyptian government to replicate his model elsewhere. But Sherif wants others to look on and learn, then do it for themselves. It's not that he's not interested in helping others, but Hemaya's work has expanded beyond its initial environmental focus to work on education, health and social issues too, leaving him little time to spare.

"Everything is related nowadays", Sherif explained, whilst talking us through his inordinate list of initiatives. He runs cleaning services which work on the streets and in the hospitals of his local towns, organises a coastal patrol for local people to protect their waters, and he funds everything from wind-mill installation to camel vaccines! If you pop down to Nuweiba, 30 kilome-tres along the coast from Basata, there are palm trees lining the harbour and an artistic fish sculpture on the roundabout as you approach – all thanks to guess who?

Schools too have benefited from Hemaya's commitment to changing the face of Sinai. With financial support from Vodafone, all local primary schools in the area recently received a facelift and now clinics are being built on-site as well. Hemaya has opened a youth centre and works with street kids. They are working on building a new playground, have just finished a new ICT cen-tre and have plans to open a women's empowerment project in the months ahead. The list could go on... crazy, hey? No wonder the Schwab Foundation awarded Sherif Egypt's Social Entrepreneur of the Year award in 2008. But for us, two big questions linger: Where does Sherif get this much funding from? And why isn't the local government picking up more of the slack?

When it comes to raising cash, Sherif admits that money isn't a barrier. Until recently, the waste management business turned a tidy profit which was all re-invested in Hemaya's activities. Although constant fluctuations in the sell-ing price of recyclable goods make profitability difficult to predict, Sherif still isn't worried about raising the money he needs. He has plenty of wealthy friends who are easily persuadable, especially when Sherif lays on the charm. His main bugbear, however, is finding the time to do it all – something we've seen across most projects. "It's not difficult to get the money but raising money is a profession and I struggle to find the time."

When it comes to the government, there's a medley of reasons why Sherif is left to do all the work – complacency, bureaucracy and corruption included. "As long as they see someone doing it, they do nothing. But if I stopped they still wouldn't act", said Sherif. This could be interpreted as a man justify-ing his own social crusade, but Sherif has evidence to back up his claims. A few years ago, a dispute with a local governor caused him to cease his waste removal services in Dahab – a tourist town 150 kilometres further down the coast. Within a year, Dahab's streets were a disaster. The mayor was sacked and Sherif was begged to come back.

Of course we had to ask Sherif if he could ever see himself moving into poli-tics; after all the revolution is meant to have cleared space for a new breed of leaders. The answer was clear and went something like this, "Not at all, ever". Whilst Sherif supported the revolution, he's had too many run-ins with the state to forgive and forget. Over the last few decades he's been accused of being a Mossad spy and Mubarak's son was rumoured to have had his eye on Sherif's land. Anyone who poses a threat to Basata (sons of military dictators included) should know what they've got themselves into. Not a man to mince his words, Sherif made it clear what action he was prepared to take: "If any-one tries to take my land I will kill them."

Nuweiba town

A new computer lab
provided by Hemaya

As you can tell, Sherif is a tough bloke you don't want to mess with. We're not just referring to his personality - check out the pictures and I'm sure you'll agree he's doing pretty well for a man over 50! But Sherif is as soft as he is solid. He greets his guests with hugs, brims with pride about his country, always focuses on his family first and devotes himself to Islam. Interestingly, though he's tired of the battles he has to fight, he doesn't believe that Allah has granted him a choice in his journey. "God gives you as much power as you can use. If you can do more, it's not your right to do less."

This belief keeps Sherif grounded and his list of priorities long. But that's not to say there aren't stumbling blocks. The level of local engagement in Hemaya's projects, in particular the waste programme, is not yet where Sherif wants it to be. What's more, the local government has perfected the art of sending in swerve balls just when they're acting like they're onside. In 2010 they announced plans to build a monstrous power plant right in the middle of Nuweiba that, not surprisingly, got Sherif's back up. With support from the community, he managed to block the deal but he admitted that the whole charade had left him prematurely aged.

The battle was worth a few grey hairs, however, as it helped Sherif to give birth to his biggest vision yet: "I have a plan. Right now Nuweiba is the worst area in Sinai but I want it to be something - a destination", he exclaimed. Nuweiba is a transit town best known for its harbour which runs regular pilgrimage trips to Mecca and stations several ocean liners. To us it was like something out of that old TV programme *Holidays from Hell*, epitomised by a camel we saw sitting outside a half finished hotel eating out of an overflowing rubbish bin. But Sherif's dream is to transform the town into a place where people choose to stay; a vibrant hub for commerce, tourism and pilgrims. He wants the new look Nuweiba to celebrate the Bedouin culture of the local people, using it as a draw card for those wanting a slice of the 'real Egypt'. "This vision is taking a lot of time but it's in my head and I can't get rid of it", said Sherif.

Whilst we were staying with Sherif we saw many sides to him. He started the mornings as a dedicated environmentalist; dressed in Speedos he would snorkel along the coral reef, picking up litter dropped from passing boats. He then transformed into resort manager and expert host; always barefoot he gave clear directions to his staff and a guided tour to every guest. In the evenings he morphed into a community leader; dressed in a traditional Bedouin outfit, he welcomed local visitors with hugs, handshakes and copious cups of mint tea. A chameleon that could change his colours in a flash, Sherif has spent his life adapting his approach to any problem which presents itself. Though he half wishes that he could slow down, he will clearly never give up. He told us with a strong sense of duty, "I can't only be one thing".

For more info visit:

Basata: **www.basata.com**
Hemaya: **www.hemaya.org**

In Conclusion

It took us four months to cover the staggering 7890 miles from Cape Town to Cairo. Our journey took us through 11 countries and we used every imaginable mode of transport - buses, mini-vans, trains, planes, motorbikes, taxis and bicycles. We travelled in the daylight and through the dark of night, in dripping hot temperatures and miserable cold rain, through bustling industrial cities and across sparse arid plains. We ate afternoon tea by Victoria Falls, walked with lions in the South Luangwa National Park, went white water rafting on the Nile, and climbed inside Egyptian tombs. So naturally since coming home we've been asked countless times: "What was the highlight of the trip?" In response, we rarely mention the sights, scenes and sounds. Instead we find ourselves talking about the incredible people we met who far surpassed anything on the 'tourist tick list'.

When we started out on this journey, we had an idea in our minds of what makes someone a social entrepreneur. In our introduction we described them as people who bring innovative solutions to society's most pressing social and environmental challenges. Having critiqued 19 people and their projects, we stand by this definition. We found people addressing every kind of issue with every imaginable solution, many of which we considered not only innovative but also ingenious. Among our favourites were playground roundabouts that pump water, rats that sniff out landmines and Coca-Cola crates that carry medical aid.

We also characterised social entrepreneurs as being capable of breaking free from traditional business, charity or institutional structures – another premise which we think holds true. In fact most social entrepreneurs we met were very vocal about trying to break the status quo. A lot of them were purposefully trying to counter their own negative experiences of working with or within conventional international NGOs and were candid in their criticisms. Whether you agree with their opinions or not, the strength of people's disenchantment was striking. You might argue that this is a case of social entrepreneurs seeking to justify their own approach when really they're just mavericks who would always be intent on doing things their own way. But we found their points well-argued and their desire to do things differently both refreshing and incredibly brave.

Taking on big challenges that other organisations have already spent years trying to crack takes guts, especially when you consider that in developed countries this responsibility would usually fall on the state.

We had numerous conversations about the role (or lack of role) that African governments play in addressing the social and environmental issues directly affecting their countries. In the UK, we pay our taxes and in return we receive, among other things, life-saving medicines, high-quality education, regular rubbish collections and immediate access to water. In many African countries the governments not only fail to deliver such basic provisions, but they often stand in the way of those trying to do it in their place. At the most extreme end of this scale you find people like Raghda who have been interrogated and detained simply for pursuing a social cause.

When you consider the obstacles, it's unsurprising that most social entrepreneurs admitted to us that there had been moments where they'd seriously considered giving up. And yet nine times out of ten, they had kept going. We found the courage they had in their own convictions quite astounding and were shocked at how many of them had put their lives on the line to stand up for their cause. The most moving example was Betty Makoni. She knew that her actions were placing her life in Zimbabwe at risk, but she carried on regardless. Despite now living in exile, Betty's more ambitious than ever about driving a movement that stands up for the rights of girls around the globe.

Betty's story demonstrates just how dedicated social entrepreneurs can be. They all seemed to have incredibly high reserves of energy that kept them working through evenings and weekends - a characteristic you see with successful people in all fields. Some appeared superhuman - Peter Sinkamba sleeps for an average of only four hours! What was more interesting, however, was exploring the root cause of their motivation for working this hard. Usually, there was something very personal spurring them on, such as an important person, a poignant experience, a deeply held belief or a passionate hobby. Occasionally, however, it was something less emotionally charged. Charles Maisel is clearly an 'innovation addict' and Trevor Field a born salesman, skills that they have brought to their respective causes with great effect.

Intriguingly, no-one we met had consciously chosen to be a social entrepreneur. It will be fascinating to observe how this changes over the years to come. With the development of university courses dedicated to social entrepreneurship, there are more people proactively choosing this as a career path; often because they simply enjoy finding innovative answers to pressing problems rather than being committed to a particular cause. Charles Maisel is a huge fan of this shift. He would tell you that becoming transfixed on one personal issue limits the impact of a social entrepreneur. If you're talented at dreaming up potential new solutions to urgent issues then he argues that it's your responsibility to work on as many problems as possible.

This is just the tip of the iceberg when it comes to analysing social entrepreneurs and their approach to creating change. We could talk about so much more... about their differing feelings about the title 'social entrepreneur', their contrasting styles of management, their ability to inspire people to buy into their particular vision and not least their general lack of arrogance despite high-level recognition. But we want to remain true to our goal of s*howcasing* social entrepreneurship. This is a set of inspirational stories that showcase the true meaning of social entrepreneurship, rather than an academic critique or a dry list of meaningless themes.

We also wanted our stories to demonstrate that Africa is truly 'on the up'. Most of us know very little about the continent other than the names of safari parks such as the Serengeti, tragic events such as the genocide in Rwanda or contentious political figures such as President Mugabe in Zimbabwe. It was very odd travelling through Africa at the same time as watching the international news headlines on tourist abductions in Kenya, election disputes in the Ivory Coast, terrorist atrocities in Nigeria, and Arab uprisings in Tunisia, Libya and Egypt. There were endless accounts of regional conflicts and yet on the ground we were experiencing nothing of it for ourselves – a measure of how the daily triumphs of millions of Africans become eclipsed by negative press.

For our part, we were received with warmth and without question. We were invited to eat with strangers, offered free lifts to our hotels, ushered across border crossings with nothing more than a stamp in our passports and invited to join our hosts in prayer. We were uplifted by people's great spirit and their propensity to collapse into fits of laughter at even the smallest jokes. If the pace of life could feel frustratingly slow at times somehow it didn't matter because we learnt to accept that everyone was moving in tune with a different understanding of time. Looking back it seems impossible to believe but we can honestly say that every social entrepreneur we met welcomed us into their world with open arms.

To us this is testimony to the caring, sharing nature of Africa and the generosity of so many who call it their home. It is our hope, therefore, that this collection of good news stories about progress in Africa will remain with you so that next time you hear something negative about its peoples, you will be able to bring a new perspective.

Next Steps...
for you and for us

We were thrilled to hear along our journey that it wasn't just us who were being wowed by the people we were profiling. Comments from our Facebook group and on the website testified to the impact they have been making:

In response to the KickStart story, Peter wrote: "This article is indeed a reflection of what Africa can become... it only takes action to turn things around."

Gillian was moved to write about Bart Weetjans at APOPO: "What an incredible story. It is so inspiring to read about such an innovative approach as this."

Charles Maisel at Innovation Shack prompted Kevin to write: "I'm heading out to buy The Guardian, The Times, The Telegraph - sod it, I'll even buy The Sun - you just never know where that inspiration might come from!"

We hope that these stories have provoked a feeling of 'elevation' and have inspired you to think about the role *you* could play in driving change. We know that taking action may not always appear easy. There is a great long list of reasons why we often choose not to worry about the wider world. We tell ourselves: "Someone else is paid to do that", "The world has always suffered", "It's the government's responsibility", or "I'm too tired to think about anything but work". However, many of us would like to live in a place where more people feel compelled to search for answers to the world's most pressing challenges. In order to achieve this, we need to shift our mindset:

From...	*To...*
Big issues are too difficult to fix.	We can solve issues at scale.
It's up to others to solve our problems.	It's up to me/us to make change.
The world has always suffered.	We can re-write the future.

For some people these leaps in thinking will appear onerous, for others they will strike a chord. If you're in the former group, you may not have even read this far. But if you fall into the latter group, then you're the ones we want to support.

Below is a list that offers practical suggestions for ways in which you can go about making a difference. We'd hedge our bets that many of you are already taking action to support the causes you care about but, to be safe, we've tried to cover all bases. You'll notice that we're not suggesting that everyone quits their job and becomes a full-time social entrepreneur. It is, after all, only one of many ways to be a change-maker. We hope that, at the very least, these ideas will prove thought-provoking and will encourage you to consider your next steps.

EXPLORE. It's important to understand which causes matter to you most. Which person or project in this book resonated with you and why? Was it the cause, the personality, the approach? We'd encourage you to go away and learn more about the individuals and organisations that interest you. Some easy ways to act include... reading another book, signing up to a newsletter or clicking through the list of resources we have compiled for you online. If possible, try to create opportunities to visit projects in person – they will welcome people genuinely interested in their work.

SHARE. If you've been inspired by someone you've read about then take the time to pass on their story to others. If you're not sure who to tell then look for groups of like-minded people. A good place to start would be to voice your opinions on our website or post a message on our Facebook page **www.facebook.com/ontheupcapetocairo**. Or even better, log onto your own Facebook and Twitter accounts (if you have them) and demonstrate your support for organisations you respect – 'like' their Facebook group, re-post their messages or tweet about their news to your friends. And when you're finished with this book please be sure to pass it on to a friend.

GIVE. Invisible Children from Uganda have a great message around giving: Give Talent, Give Time, Give Money. Let's face it, giving cash is the easiest option and it's probably something you do already. So think about how you can step it up. What skills do you have to offer? Could you lend your business expertise to another organisation free of charge? Could you use your leadership skills by sitting on a board of trustees? Could you apply your caring side to a role as a front-line volunteer?

DARE. If you have an idea for a new way of driving social and/or environmental change, then please don't sit on it. Plan it out, talk it through and find a way to make it happen. If it means you're going to have to take some big risks such as quitting your job, raiding your savings or moving back in with your parents, then of course think carefully first. If you don't enjoy the buzz of living that close to the edge, find a partner to come along with you on the journey or someone else to take the lead. Listen to the sceptics who want to challenge your idea but use their negativity to refine your thinking and don't let them put you off.

WORK. Finding a job that has a positive social/environmental impact doesn't mean you can only work in the public or charity sectors. Jobs in the private sector with a social slant, such as social finance, social impact consultancy and corporate social responsibility, are increasingly becoming available. Any job that focuses on people or the planet before profit is probably going to pay you less than working in the mainstream corporate world, but if you want a job with more of a social purpose then take a look at all the options and you might even be pleasantly surprised by what you can earn.

INFLUENCE. If you're happy with your job then why not think about how you can influence your workplace from the inside. Wherever you work there are plenty of ways that you could push for positive change such as challenging the ethics of your suppliers, encouraging the recruitment of staff from less advantaged backgrounds, reducing the carbon footprint of the organisation or business and persuading your team to lend a percentage of its time to a good cause. Many professional organisations give their employees the opportunity to undertake 'pro bono' work – if the offer is there then make the most of it.

Our website has a huge list of links under External Resources that we've pulled together to help you. Visit **www.ontheup.org** to browse the links and please let us know if you think there are important resources that should be added.

As for us, we're celebrating that our marriage has survived two massive tests: months of living in each other's pockets and co-authoring a book. We're slowly getting back into the groove of returning to full-time jobs, though we often pine to be back in Africa. Most of our spare time is dedicated to sharing On the Up with as many people as possible. If there's a genuine demand for On the Up, Part Two, we'd love to make it happen. We'd gladly take another trip ourselves but even better, we'd love other people to start their own On the Up adventures. If you fancy exploring other world routes and discovering more inspirational stories, then let us know. Perhaps together we can grow On the Up into a social enterprise of its own.

Notes

Most of the quotations and reporting in this book derive from our own interviews with the social entrepreneurs who were profiled. They provided us with facts and figures that demonstrated the scale and success of their operations. This notes section highlights the key resources we used to gather broader information about Africa. We have also tried to reference interesting organisations and initiatives that the reader might want to learn more about.

A note on statistics:
All the country statistics featured in the country data are from CIA World Fact book (see **www.cia.gov**), apart from the IMF country ranking. All GDP statistics are based on purchasing power parity. There is no accurate data for South Sudan in this area.

Introduction

1   See **www.wcmt.org.uk**
2   Jonathan Haidt, *Happiness Hypothesis: Finding Modern Truth in Ancient Wisdom* (Basic Books, 2006)
3   See **www.greatergood.berkeley.edu/article/item/wired_to_be_inspired**
4   See **www.reprieve.org.uk**
5   See **www.nspcc.org.uk**
6   See **www.payyourway.org.uk/special-focus/charity**
7   See **www.skills-thirdsector.org.uk/documents/The_UK_Voluntary_Workforce_Almanac_2011.pdf**
8   See **www.redcross.org.uk**
9   See **www.dfid.gov.uk**
10 See **www.ashoka.org**
11 See, for example: Alex Nicholls, *Social Entrepreneurship: New Models of Sustainable Social Change* (Oxford University Press, 2006); David Bornstein, *How to Change the World: Social Entrepreneurs and the Power of New Ideas* (Oxford University Press, 2007); David Bornstein and Susan David, *Social Entrepreneurship: What Everyone Needs to Know* (Oxford University Press, 2010)
12 See **www.schwabfound.org**
13 See **www.skollfoundation.org**
14 *United Nations, World Population Prospects: The 2010 Revision* (Department of Economic and Social Affairs, Population Division)
15 Organisation for Economic Co-operation and Development (OECD), Stat Extracts (2011)
16 International Monetary Fund (IMF), *Regional Economic Outlook Sub-Saharan Africa: Weathering the Storm* (2010)
17 McKinsey Global Institute, *Fulfilling the Promise of Sub-Saharan Africa* (2010)
18 Africa Progress Panel, *The Transformative Power of Partnerships, Africa Progress Report* (2011)
19 See **www.un.org/millenniumgoals**
20 United Nations, *World Population Prospects* (2011 revision)
21 United Nations, *The Millennium Development Goals Report* (2010)
22 See **www.indexmundi.com**
23 United Nations Development Programme, *Human Development Report* (2010)

24 United Nations Educational, Scientific and Cultural Organisation (UNESCO), *EFA Global Monitoring Report: The Hidden Crisis - Armed Conflict and Education* (2011)

25 See One International's Living Proof Report: **www.one.org/livingproof/ en/article/progress-in-education**

26 Africa Progress Panel, *The Transformative Power of Partnerships, Africa Progress Report* (2011)

27 See **www.indexmundi.com**

South Africa

28 See **www.indexmundi.com/south_africa/unemployment_rate.html**

29 Ashoka Fellowships are awarded to the world's leading social entrepreneurs. To date Ashoka has recognised nearly 3,000 Fellows globally, providing them with financial and strategic support to scale their ideas.

30 The World Health Organisation, *Guidelines on the provision of Manual Wheelchairs in less resourced settings* (2008)

31 See **www.msafirimuzungu.wordpress.com/2010/04/27/imported-wheelchair-graveyard** for a photo of 'wheelchair graveyards'

32 John Elkington and Pamela Hartigan, *The Power of Unreasonable People: How Social Entrepreneurs Create Markets that Change the World* (Harvard Business Review Press, 2008) p.37-42

33 Matthew Bishop and Michael Green, *Philanthrocapitalism: How Giving can Save the World* (A & C Black, 2008)

34 United Nations, *The Millennium Development Goals Report* (2010)

35 See **www.onedifference.org//food-drink/water**

36 See **www.acts.co.za/tax/30__public_benefit_organisations.htm**

37 See **www.wbi.worldbank.org/developmentmarketplace**

Zimbabwe

38 See **www.avert.org/cure-for-aids.htm**

39 See **www.edition.cnn.com/SPECIALS/cnn.heroes/archive09/betty. makoni.html**

40 See **www.oxfam.org.uk**

41 See **www.actionagainsthunger.org/blog/letter-asks-ngos-leave-zimbabwe**

42 See **www.aiesec.org**

43 See **www.thehubnetwork.co.uk**

44 See **www.weforum.org/community/forum-young-global-leaders**

Zambia

45 UN Inter-agency Group on Child Mortality Estimation, Levels and Trends in Child Mortality (2011)

46 See World Bank Data Indicators **www.data.worldbank.org/indicator/ SH.DYN.MORT?page=5**

47 See **www.businesscalltoaction.org**

48 See **www.colalife.org/tag/eddie-mair**

49 See **www.sabmiller.com** and **www.unicef.org**

50 See **www.jnj.com**

51 See **www.changemakers.com** for Ashoka Changemakers – an online platform to find and reward great social innovations.
52 The Environment Protection Fund in Zambia was set up under the Mines and Minerals Development Act and mining companies working in Zambia make statutory payments into it. The fund has been set up to ensure that all mining companies execute their environmental protection and rehabilitation responsibilities as required by law and to protect the government in case companies do not adhere.
53 See **www.oecd.org/dataoecd/56/36/1922428.pdf** for OECD Guidelines for Multinational Enterprises; see **http://www2.ohchr.org/english/law/ cescr.htm** for the UN's International Covenant on Economic, Social and Cultural Rights
54 See **www.ohchr.org/english/bodies/hrcouncil** for UN Human Rights Council; see **http://www.bis.gov.uk/** for the re-named Department of Trade & Industry, the Department for Business, Skills and Innovation
55 See **www.glencore.com** for information about Mopani Copper Mine
56 See **www.afdb.org/en** for African Development Bank Group; see **http:// www.worldbank.org/** for the World Bank; see **www.un.org** for the United Nations

Tanzania

57 See **www.listverse.com/2008/08/11/10-countries-with-the-most- landmines** for the world's top 10 landmine affected countries
58 See **www.the-monitor.org/index.php/LM/The-Issues/Mine-Ban-Treaty** for more information about the Mine Ban Treaty
59 See **www.mineactionstandards.org/international-standards/imas-in- english/about-imas**
60 See **www.who.int/mediacentre/news/releases/2005/africa_ emergency/en/index.html**
61 World Health Organisation (WHO), Global TB Control (2011)
62 See **www.who.int/mediacentre/factsheets/fs104/en/**
63 United Nations Educational, Scientific and Cultural Organisation (UNESCO), *EFA Global Monitoring Report: The Hidden Crisis – Armed Conflict and Education* (2011)
64 Africa Progress Panel, *The Transformative Power of Partnerships, Africa Progress Report* (2011)
65 African Development Bank (AfDB), African Union (AU), United Nations Economic Commission for Africa (UNECA) and United Nations Development Programme (UNDP), Assessing Progress in Africa toward the Millennium Development Goals (2010)
66 See **www.hewlett.org** for the Hewlett Foundation and **www.sida.se/ English** for the Swedish International Development Agency
67 **www.opengovpartnership.org**

Rwanda

68 Africa Recovery, Vol. 12 (August 1998) p. 4, and **www.survivors-fund. org.uk/resources/rwandan-history/statistics**
69 Catharine Newbury and Hannah Baldwin, U.S. Agency for International Development, *Aftermath: Women in Postgenocide Rwanda* (2000)
70 See **www.foundationrwanda.org** and **www.amnesty.org/en/library/ asset/AFR47/007/2004/en/53d74ceb-d5f7-11dd-bb24-1fb85fe8fa05/ afr470072004en.pdf**, page 2
71 Rwandan Ministry of Social Affairs, Census in 2007

Uganda

72 See **http://www.hospiceafrica.or.ug/**
73 Uganda Prisons Service operate an open door policy that enables members of the public, human rights activists and investigators to visit prison premises.
74 See **www.deathpenaltyproject.org/content_pages/31**
75 Institute for Economics & Peace (2010) and The Global Peace Index (2010)
76 *World Development Report: Conflict, Security and Development* (2011)

Kenya

77 See **www.unwater.org/statistics_san.html**
78 See **www.worldvision.org**
79 See **www.acumenfund.org**
80 See **www.weforum.org** for World Economic Forum; see **www. clintonglobalinitiative.org** for Global Clinton Initiative; **www. worldtoilet.org/wto/** for World Toilet Organisation; and **www. globalwaterchallenge.org** for Global Water Challenge
81 United Nations, *The Millennium Development Goals Report* (2010)
82 See **www.vso.org.uk**
83 See IDE **www.ideorg.org/OurTechnologies/Home.aspx**; SK Industries **www.skipumps.com/treadle.htm**; Practical Action **www. practicalaction.org/irrigation-techniques-1**
84 Food and Agriculture Organisation of the United Nations (FAO), *Treadle Pumps in Africa* (2000)
85 International Food Policy Research Institute (2010), *Global Hunger Index* (2010)
86 See **www.fao.org/english/newsroom/highlights/2001/010103-e.htm**
87 See **www.gatesfoundation.org**
88 See **www.news.bbc.co.uk/1/hi/world/africa/7344816.stm** and **www. news.bbc.co.uk/1/hi/world/africa/7174670.stm**
89 See **www.google.com/adplanner/static/top1000/#**
90 See **www.ted.com**

South Sudan

91 U.S. Committee for Refugees (2001)
92 See www.unicef.org/sowc96/closboys.htm
93 UNESCO Policy Paper: *Building a better future: Education for an Independent South Sudan* (2011)
94 See www.cilt.org.uk/home/research_and_statistics/statistics/secondary_education/secondary_schools_in_uk
95 See www.ifdc.org/Nations/South_Sudan

Egypt

96 See www.en.wikipedia.org/wiki/Economy_of_Egypt
97 See www.moneyweek.com/blog/merryn-somerset-webb-egypt-youth-unemployment-and-britain-00311
98 World Bank Indicators (2010)